Build with the Lord

pastoral advice for prayer groups in the charismatic renewal

By Bert Ghezzi

to my brothers and sisters
in the Grand Haven, Michigan, prayer group

Published by: Word of Life
P.O. Box 331
Ann Arbor, Michigan 48107

Printed in the United States of America

Contents

Introduction

The Prayer Group in the Charismatic Renewal

Unlike several past charismatic outbursts which flared, died, and left no significant heritage, the modern-day charismatic renewal promises to permanently enrich the life of the church. The renewal's extraordinary success and promise is due chiefly to the success of the prayer group.

Prayer groups are gatherings of men and women whose lives are centered on the Lord Jesus and whose relationships are built around a prayer meeting and other shared activities. Praying together in groups is certainly no novelty. Throughout the centuries, Christian men and women have always gathered in groups to pray and share the mighty deeds of God. What is new, however, is the extent to which charismatic prayer groups have begun to spread throughout the Christian world. *The Directory of Catholic Charismatic Prayer Groups* for 1975 lists more than 2300 prayer groups in the United States and more than 1500 groups in 53 other countries. Also new to this age is the free flow of praise, song, sharing, and spiritual gifts which typifies charismatic prayer meetings.

Prayer groups are the means by which the charismatic renewal spreads. They frequently have a powerful impact on individuals. For many people, the initial contact with a prayer group involves a new personal encounter with the Lord. Subsequent weekly gatherings for praise, teaching, and sharing provide persons with continuing support for personal growth.

I say this with conviction, for prayer meetings changed my life. It was through the first charismatic prayer meetings at the University of Notre Dame that the Lord laid hold of me and shook me free of the doubts and gloom which had oppressed me for years. Since those March evenings in 1967, weekly prayer meetings have been the context for my moving ahead with the Lord and growing in the Christian life. The Grand Haven, Michigan prayer group, which began a year after I moved to that city in 1967, brought me together with men and women who cared for me. With them I learned to praise God freely; I grew in knowing how to receive guidance from the Lord; I began to discover how to serve others and how to allow others to love, encourage, and correct me. As I came to know that I was accepted in the prayer group as a brother, I was healed of a lingering sense of self-hatred, which is now completely gone. In short, the Lord has used prayer groups to change everything in my life for the better. He seems to be doing the same for thousands of others. He is employing the spiritual dynamic of prayer groups to bring his people to love him and to aid them in their spiritual growth.

A movement like the charismatic renewal is somewhat like a modern building. Both must be flexible enough to adapt to changing needs, yet must have the structure and stability to make them durable. Buildings of sticks or straw just blow away without fulfilling their purpose. A movement without structure and identity ceases to be a movement. A well-designed building is adaptable to the different needs of many owners and tenants. Movements also need to be adaptable to many local situations. The prayer group achieves this balance between flexibility and structure. It is the "living stone" of the charismatic renewal.

The great variety of prayer groups in the charismatic renewal testifies to its exceptional flexibility. Over the past eight years, prayer groups have been molded in response to differing local situations and needs. Therefore, they differ significantly in size, composition, extent, and structure. Five dedicated men and women constitute a prayer group at a university in the Southwest, while the Servants of the Light Community in Minneapolis-St. Paul sponsors a weekly prayer gathering with more than 1,000 participants. According to the current *Directory,* most groups seem to have more than 20 but fewer than 150 members. Prayer groups are springing up within Catholic parishes in New Orleans, Grand Rapids, Pittsburgh, and elsewhere. Other groups, such as the one in Grand Haven, are ecumenical in character, serving members of local Catholic and Protestant churches. These ecumenical prayer groups are becoming commonplace in the charismatic renewal and seem to be making a significant contribution to a grass roots ecumenism. Finally, some prayer groups grow out of the needs of certain people: priests who gather to pray over the Scriptures as they prepare Sunday sermons; workingmen who spend lunch hours together in prayer; wives whose husbands are not active in the movement who gather in morning prayer groups; teen-agers, children, and others who form their own prayer meetings.

A strength of the prayer group is its ability to change. Individual groups often undergo significant transitions in a few short years. The Grand Rapids, Michigan, prayer group began as a house meeting in November, 1967. Within two months, the membership had swollen and the group divided, one part serving the Aquinas College community and nearby parishes, and the other serving the west side of Grand Rapids. Later, both groups merged into a large center which introduced the charismatic renewal into Western Michigan. In the past several years, the big prayer meeting has been diminishing in size and numerous smaller parish prayer groups have appeared. These changes in the prayer group reflect in part the changing needs of the Grand Rapids situation. The Grand Rapids prayer groups is typical of many. Because prayer groups can evolve to meet changing needs, the charismatic renewal can become relevant everywhere without freezing into rigid patterns.

At the same time, prayer groups have enough stability to make the charismatic renewal durable. In most groups, a faithful core of members comes together and allows the Lord to build something among them. These participants freely make an adult commitment to live for the Lord and they undertake some kind of commitment, often unarticulated, to each other. The Grand Haven group in this regard is typical of thousands of others. In 1968, two couples began to pray together every week. Within two years about 35 people had joined them. By 1975, the prayer group had undergone a number of important changes. The size of the group had increased to about 200 persons. Its composition changed from all Catholic to ecumenical. At one point, the Grand Haven group carefully divided to start a new prayer group in Muskegon, Michigan, 20 miles north of Grand Haven, in order to serve that area more effectively. In the midst of all this, the Grand Haven prayer group remained stable because of the faithfulness of its members. Most of the original 35 members and many of the hundreds of others who shared the life of the group are still associated with the group. The minimal expectations of membership—attendance at weekly prayer meetings and a service such as setting up chairs or leading discussions—are eagerly fulfilled in the Grand Haven prayer group. The Holy Spirit has effortlessly created this kind of faithfulness in prayer groups everywhere. Because prayer group members make a priority of coming together before the Lord in prayer, he has been able to assemble a vast network of prayer groups in the charismatic renewal.

Prayer groups are genuine gifts from God, but they do not fall out of the sky fully developed. They are built by men in association with the Lord. The charismatic renewal is accumulating a body of practical advice about constructing effective prayer groups. This book is essentially an effort to share that advice so that all of us can build with the Lord more effectively.

Five essential areas need constant attention if our prayer groups are to be built in the Lord: 1) the prayer meeting; 2) leadership; 3) a way of helping others receive new life; 4) sound teaching; and 5) relationships among participants.

1) Effective Prayer Meetings. Prayer meetings are inspired by the Holy Spirit, but a healthy prayer meeting does not happen automatically when people gather for prayer. Prayer groups founder when they lack an effective vehicle for group praise. We need to learn how to develop prayer meetings that properly honor the Lord and foster Christian growth.

2) Leadership. Healthy prayer groups have some kind of identifiable leadership. The smallest, least organized group needs someone to take a concern for its life, even if the job is simply to start and stop the prayer meeting and to see to it that someone provides coffee afterwards. Larger groups with more activities and deeper commitments need more developed leadership.

3) A Way to Help Others Receive New Life. The Lord expects prayer groups to take responsibility for new people that he brings to them. He does not want us to treat new people casually. Prayer groups which have agreed on some orderly way to help people receive new life from the Lord have benefitted both in growth and stability.

4) Sound Teaching. Responsible prayer groups help their participants receive sound basic instruction in the Christian life. The Lord baptizes people in the Holy Spirit so that they might have the power and freedom to become mature Christians. Prayer groups need to provide good teaching so that members may gain the Lord's wisdom which they need in order to grow. Well-instructed prayer groups remain healthy and properly oriented.

5) Relationships Among Members. Prayer groups often form around personal spiritual experience and manifestations of spiritual gifts. However, if these groups are to endure, they need to learn how to channel the power of the Holy Spirit into building sound Christian personal relationships. Spiritual gifts are worthless in prayer groups where there is back-biting, division, jealousy, self-seeking, and hatred.

This is a book about caring for these five essential areas of prayer group life. When a prayer group develops these areas properly, it is in a good position to cooperate with the Holy Spirit. The group is then like a sailboat correctly rigged, ready to raise its sails confidently into the full force of the wind. The wind catches the sails and the craft moves ahead swiftly and safely. A poorly rigged craft exposing its sails to the same wind would very likely capsize. Poorly constructed prayer groups capsize every day, a tragic waste this little book hopes to help prevent.

1

Building with the Lord

In his youth Jesus was a carpenter's assistant. At first he "helped" as most children do by playing with Joseph's tools and wood scraps. But at some point Joseph began to teach his son the principles of good construction. He showed Jesus how to follow a plan; how to select appropriate materials; how to measure and cut wood; how to choose and use tools properly; how to move from one step to the next in an orderly way; how to keep the finished product in mind. Jesus easily transferred some of these principles to his work of establishing the church. He followed a plan; he kept the finished product in mind; he proceeded in an orderly fashion; he employed sound principles of construction. Jesus was a skilled master builder, erecting the dwelling place of God among men.

The New Testament indicates that Jesus knew a great deal about building men into effective communities. He trained a small band of disciples to continue his work, just as Joseph had trained him. Jesus wanted his followers to understand and employ sound principles for bringing men together in the new Christian society.

Jesus taught his disciples that he was to lead and they were to follow him. He showed them how to rely on his power, to expect him to act as they went about their jobs of building the church. Jesus commanded the disciples to proclaim the good news; they were not to let other activities distract the church from this primary job of evangelism. Jesus showed Christians how to pattern their lives in right order. Finally, he commanded Christians to make love their aim and to do everything in love.

These are the principles of building with the Lord. Just as Joseph's principles of carpentry have been handed through the ages and are still valid today, the principles of building with the Lord have always been with the church and are still the key to its health. Today, these principles are being restored to Christian life through the promptings of the Holy Spirit.

Let Jesus Lead

One of these principles is that Jesus should lead and we should follow him in everything. Jesus did nothing in his earthly ministry apart from his Father's leading. "Truly, truly, I say to you, the Son can do nothing of his own accord, but only what he sees the Father doing; for whatever he does, that the Son does likewise" (John 5:19). In the same way, the Lord wants to direct all of our work so that we might advance *his* plan, not ours.

We can easily find ourselves doing something for God rather than allowing God to do something with us. This was a mark of my own Christian service before I became involved in the charismatic renewal. As a university student, I participated in various Christian groups—parish societies, university organizations, national movements. My associates and I worked very hard and accomplished some valuable things for church renewal. However, we proceeded in a manner which kept us from achieving more and which prevented the Lord from doing what he wanted with us.

I was involved with a university group which had determined that the school's theology curriculum and liturgical celebrations were inadequate. We dedicated ourselves to educate the campus for change. We sponsored a lecture series, bringing in top theologians and liturgists. We persuaded faculty to offer non-credit courses in theology and Scripture and volunteered to take them. We held liturgical days and pressured the chaplains to reform worship services by encouraging congregational participation.

In retrospect, I can see that we made one important mistake: we never asked the Lord to lead us. We had *our* plan to reform the school's theology and liturgy, and we set out to implement the plan in our own way. Because of this, I am not proud today of the methods and tactics we used to get our ideas accepted. We were quite political and self-determined. We would pressure and try to persuade others; if they did not agree, we would bypass them and seek another way to accomplish our ends. These were the ordinary methods of getting something done on a campus in the 1960s. Because we did not ask the Lord to lead us, we knew no other way.

I also suspect that the Lord may have had an entirely different plan for us at that time. He may have wanted us to study theology harder instead of trying to reform the curriculum. He may have wanted us to become more involved in civil rights reform rather than liturgical reform at that time. I do not know what the Lord's plan was for us then because I did not ask him.

Innocent as I may have been, this way of working was not harmless. I spent a lot of energy in what I thought was advancing the Lord's work; in fact, I was holding him back. After college, I went to graduate school and spent the first six months "high" on Jesus and working to transform the campus. I was constantly running to meetings, counseling with people, attending study sessions, and campaigning to renovate the liturgy. I did some studying for my courses, but much less than I should have. I thought I was doing something for the Lord, but I was really doing something for myself. I was following *my* plan for renewal, not the Lord's. What the Lord wanted to do for me in graduate school was to train me in the skills I would need for the long-term service he planned for me in teaching, writing, and editing. Some Christian activities were standing in his way. The Lord could not do what he wanted with me because I was too busy doing something for him.

When I was baptized in the Holy Spirit, I saw what was wrong with trying to do things for God. I began to see that the Lord was working by his own plan and through his own power to bring people together in his Spirit. He had a plan for me too. What's more, I learned that I could find out what the Lord wanted me to do by praying, listening to God, reading Scripture, sharing with brothers and sisters, and through the exercise of spiritual gifts. Over the past eight years, this principle of building *with* the Lord rather than *for* him has been a guiding precept in the work of the Christian groups I have been associated with.

I recall two examples of this principle in action in the prayer group in Grand Haven, Michigan, a group which I was part of for seven years. We thought for a while that the group was going to be an all-Catholic prayer group contributing to the life of our parish. However, through prayer, prophecy, and common reflection on our situation, the Lord redirected us and made us an ecumenical group serving a larger geographical area and many churches. Later, we thought that the Grand Haven prayer group would become a full Christian community where the members would make a full commitment of their lives to each other. The Lord showed us through teaching and experience that what he wanted was a prayer group, where the members made a more limited commitment. When we set aside *our* agenda, the Lord was able to implement *his* plan.

Servants of the Lord must decide to build *with* him. If we build *for* him we do not really serve him; we serve ourselves and obstruct him. The Lord's servants will be with him where *he* is working, allowing him to inspire, form, and guide us constantly. Wherever the Lord is, his servants will be there too (John 12:26).

Expect the Lord to Act

Another principle of building with the Lord is to expect him to act, to care for his people, to accomplish what is needed. Jesus promised: "Whatever you ask in my name I will do it, that the Father may be glorified in the Son; if you ask anything in my name I will do it" (John 14:13-14).

Before I was baptized in the Holy Spirit, I had faith in God, but it was not the kind of faith which expected the Lord to act powerfully or do important things for me because he loved me. In fact, I tended to read God's scriptural promises as though each had a footnote saying: "except Bert Ghezzi." The same attitude characterized my approach to Christian work. I prayed and worked as though everything depended on me. I actually expected God to do very little.

In my work in the charismatic renewal, I have seen vividly and repeatedly how expectant faith helps the Christian work with God. The prayer groups which I have worked with learned how to rely on God in the face of needs and difficulties, knowing that the Lord would intervene to help us. One instance I remember involved an apparent crisis in a group. After four years of meeting Wednesdays at a Knights of Columbus hall, the Grand Haven prayer group decided to change the night and place of its gathering. For a time immediately after the move, attendance dwindled. The power seemed to have evaporated from the prayer meeting. The leaders could have approached the situation with fear and worry: "maybe the Lord did not want us to move after all?" Instead we applied a basic principle we had learned: we praised God and expected him to care for the group. Within a few weeks, the prayer group had grown larger and the prayer meeting became livelier than ever. Trusting God enabled us to experience his caring for our needs. Indeed, I suspect that God allowed the group to experience these difficulties so that we could learn how to turn to him in expectant faith and then to experience his boundless love.

However, expectant faith does not mean that all we have to do is pray in order to see the Lord straighten out a problem. Sometimes deciding to "pray about it" is an unspiritual abdication of responsibility. "Praying about it" may be an unfaithful response to a situation where an active faith and direct action are called for. In most difficult situations, expectant faith means more than prayer. It means relying on God and taking confident action. Instead of ignoring difficulties, hoping that they will magically disappear, we can trust the Lord and face difficulties as they come up.

For example, simply "praying about it" would have been the wrong response when the leaders team of the Grand Haven prayer group discovered that it had lost touch with the prayer group. We had been making decisions in isolation from the realities of the group's life. This seemed to be a crisis of significant proportions which threatened to divide the prayer group. The leaders prayed and fasted, interceding for the group and expecting the Lord to work. But we also took action to correct the situation. We talked personally with all those who sensed the communications breakdown. To improve communications, we started a newsletter, published the agenda of leaders' meetings, urged people to communicate their concerns to the leaders' team, gave teachings about good communications, and established an advisory committee to give regular feedback to the leaders. Failure to act in this fashion might have harmed the prayer group. In fact, the steps we took to improve communications gave the leaders a much sounder basis for making decisions. Acting in faith helped the group improve relationships and restored its unity.

When we apply this principle of expecting the Lord to act, we do not need to feel as if we had a great quantity of faith. We need only look to the Lord with whatever quantity of faith we have, and trust him to act. The Lord is an infinite source of power who can produce great results when tapped by even a very small amount of faith. "Trust in the Lord and do good, so that you will dwell in the land, and enjoy security. Take delight in the Lord, and he will give you the desires of your heart. Commit your way to the Lord; trust in him, and he will act. He will bring forth your vindication as the light, and your right as the noonday" (Psalm 37:3-6).

Proclaim Jesus as Our Ideal

Faithfulness to proclaiming the gospel of Jesus Christ is another principle for building Christian groups wisely. "When I came to you, brethren," Paul declared to the Corinthians, "I did not come proclaiming to you the testimony of God in lofty words or wisdom. For I decided to know nothing among you except Jesus Christ and him crucified" (1 Cor. 2:1-2). The time never came when Paul could rest on his accomplishments and say "At last I'm done preaching the gospel. What next?" That time should never come for us either. Preaching the good news is not only essential for the foundation of Christian groups; it is essential for their survival.

The ideal of Jesus Christ is also the foundation of every Christian's life. Unlike the foundation of a building, the foundation of our lives needs to be strengthened every day. We need to be continually confronted with a proclamation of the lordship of Jesus Christ. We need to continually realize that Jesus is our ideal, the one who saves us, the one for whom we live. Otherwise, our foundation will quickly fall into disrepair and may even collapse in some places. The liturgy of the church understands this well. This is the reason the proclamation of the Word holds a central place in the mass and other Christian worship services. One reason for the sustained vitality of the charismatic renewal is the participants' singlehearted zeal to live for and proclaim Jesus in their daily lives.

To build with the Lord, we must clearly realize that our hearts are set on him. All of our decisions are crucially affected by the ideal we live for. If our sole objective is making money, that will influence our decisions about money. Should I invest all my income in stocks or to use it to pay the bills of a poor family next door? Astute businessmen know that success depends on single-minded pursuit of their goal. When the president of Avis decided that his company should become the fastest-growing rent-a-car chain, he eliminated everything else that got in the way. He sold all the company's motels, hotels, airlines, and other subsidiaries which had little or nothing to do with the rent-a-car business. He put a sign by his phone: "Is what I am doing or about to do getting us closer to our objective?" The sign stopped him from making many commitments, phone calls, and trips which might have sidetracked him from his single-minded purpose.

A person's decision to live for God ought to cut through everything else and should influence his decisions in the same way that profits motivated the people at Avis. Because it is easy for us to get sidetracked, we need to have constant reminders of who it is we are living for. The Avis people had to remind each other of their objective continually or they would have lost sight of it. Similarly, we need little interior signs which read: "Is what I am doing or about to do getting me closer to the Lord?" And so we dare not cease preaching the gospel. We must always proclaim Jesus Christ as our ideal, our goal, the source of our life.

To date the charismatic renewal has been employing this principle. Observers at charismatic prayer meetings are sometimes surprised that, while there often may be no mention of the Holy Spirit, scarcely anything happens which does not proclaim Jesus. Individual participants in prayer groups are regularly confronted with the clear sharp sword of the gospel which cuts away at the things which creep into our hearts and compete with the Lord for first place.

When Christian movements cease to apply this principle they soon cease to be healthy movements. I have worked with several movements in the Catholic Church where this has happened. Each started out singlemindedly to advance the causes of Jesus Christ; somewhere along the way the goal became clouded. Other purposes crowded in beside the original goal of proclaiming Jesus until this goal was no longer distinguishable from the newcomers. The new goals were not evil or un-Christian. But they were not *Jesus* and that was what was wrong with them.

Prayer groups which are foundering ought to look at their foundation. If they are not proclaiming Jesus, they are wandering from their objective. "According to the commission of God given to me," said Paul, "like a skilled master builder I laid a foundation, and another man is building upon it. Let each man take care how he builds upon it. For no other foundation can any one lay than that which is laid, which is Jesus Christ" (1 Cor. 3:10-11).

Pattern Our Lives

Another principle for building with the Lord is to structure our relationships and activities so that they are in good order. This was the thrust of Paul's correction of the Christian assembly at Corinth. The Corinthians were tolerating disordered relationships and wild meetings; these caused confusion and persuaded unbelievers that Christianity was not credible. Paul insisted that the Corinthians establish order in their personal relationships: people in bad sexual relationships were to be corrected (1 Cor. 5). He demanded that they bring a pattern into their gatherings, establishing an order for their worship services (1 Cor. 11:2-14:40). Near the conclusion of his guidelines for Corinthian prayer meetings, Paul explained the reason for them: "For you can all prophesy one by one, so that all may learn and all be encouraged; and the spirits of prophets are subject to prophets. For God is not a God of confusion but of peace'' (1 Cor. 14:31-33). Interestingly, the Greek word for ''peace'' in this passage also means ''order.'' The Lord calls us to good order, because he wants us to be at peace.

Modern men do not always associate order and peace. Some people have had bad experiences with an abusive, rigid order, and falsely assume that order is the enemy of freedom and creativity. If we have been hurt by a wrong approach to order, the Lord will heal us if we ask. The truth is that order creates a framework—a pattern—which allows greater freedom. Unrestrained spontaneity—the absence of all order—is freedom's real enemy. A novice who wants to play the violin but deliberately chooses not to practice and not to follow musical rules

will soon discover he does not have the freedom to make good music. He is free only to make noise. The novice who practices four hours a day for ten years and masters all the rules eventually becomes free to be spontaneous and creative. This principle holds in our personal lives and in our groups. To be free, we need order. To build creatively with the Lord, we need to structure our lives according to his truth.

In the early days of the charismatic renewal, few prayer groups I attended had any deliberate structure. In fact, we would probably have resisted any formal pattern as unspiritual. However, we did have acknowledged leaders who started and stopped meetings. After a few months—and some very long and wild prayer meetings—we began to see that order was indeed the desire of the Holy Spirit for us. For example, it was our practice at first to invite anyone who wished to come forward and be prayed with for being baptized in the Holy Spirit. We soon learned that many people who did this had psychological problems and needed help we were not offering; others had bad experiences; some skeptics went away in mocking disbelief. We corrected this situation by establishing order. We agreed to have an explanation session after the meeting to tell people what was happening and to

prepare and instruct those who desired to receive a release of the Holy Spirit. We decided not to pray for anyone who had not heard the explanation. Later we began using the seven-week Life in the Spirit Seminars to lead people to this new relationship with God.

Establishing explanation talks and setting up orderly ways of helping people receive the baptism in the Holy Spirit was very important to the group and to new people. These were structures which enabled us to serve those the Lord sent to us. These structures helped us grow, because we were able to build good relations with those we helped. People benefitted from these structures and became permanent members of the group.

Some subsequent decisions which seemed quite small brought large results. We discovered we did not have to meet until 2 a.m. and decided to end our prayer meetings at a considerably earlier time. This enabled us to get sufficient rest so that we could be responsible parents, students, and employees during the day. The prayer meetings themselves improved as we encouraged the leader to become more directive. We decided to have a prayer room after the meeting where people could receive prayer for personal needs. This opened the prayer meeting for more praise and less petition and gave people who needed it an opportunity for personal attention afterwards. Perhaps the single most important structure was the identification and acceptance of a team of leaders who took responsibility over all of our shared activities. This ensured that everyone and everything would get proper care and that we would stick to our agreements.

Some are inclined to regard the adoption of structures such as these as abandoning the Spirit and "returning to the Law." However, I am convinced that the impulse to pattern the lives of our groups is a leading of the Holy Spirit, an expression of a desire close to the heart of God. Jesus is the cornerstone of the dwelling of God among men; the Lord wants everything aligned on him so that we might manifest the unity which will bring faith to the world (Eph. 2:20; John 17:21). This holds true both for the church and for prayer groups within the church.

Make Love Your Aim

The principle which has preeminence among all the others is Jesus' new command: "Love one another; even as I have loved you, that you also love one another. By this all men will know that you are my disciples, if you have love for one another" (John 13:34-35). Without brotherly love we cannot build with the Lord, and none of the other principles can function properly. The reason for this is simple: love is not merely a way of building with God; love is God's purpose. When he created and redeemed us, God intended to draw us into a loving union with each other in Jesus. The dwelling God is building among men is love. Therefore, all of our work must be done both in love and for love.

I am deceiving myself if I claim to follow Jesus, expect God to act, preach the good news tirelessly, or bring everything into God's right order, and yet have no love. "If any one says, 'I love God,' and hates his brother, he is a liar; for he who does not love his brother whom he has seen, cannot love God whom he has not seen. And this commandment we have from him, that he who loves God should love his brother also" (1 John 4:20-21). I can spend my last drop of energy, time, and money building prayer groups, but if I have no love, I have not accomplished anything. Far from pleasing the Lord, I will have earned his just rejection (See Matt. 7:21-23).

I learned this lesson when I proposed a very elaborate reorganization to the other leaders of the Grand Haven prayer group. My plan was a complex system which set up structures for supervising all of our activities. In addition, I suggested a more aggressive approach to meetings; for example, I wanted to have the leaders of the services meet weekly. Further, I wanted the group to establish an advisory council which would meet monthly. I had a multitude of great organizational ideas; the other leaders had a great deal of patience. For a time, there was an unspoken sense among them that something was lacking in all my ideas for restructuring.

I was corrected by one of the women who handed me a cassette copy of a talk she had heard at a leaders conference; she insisted that I listen to it. The talk revolutionized my understanding, and changed the life of our prayer group. The speaker's point was that while the Lord wanted us to structure our groups wisely, he wanted us to direct everything toward the goal of becoming brother and sisters. The number and kind of meetings must be shaped by that end; they must not become ends in themselves. I have rarely been so excited by a talk. Through this talk, the other leaders and I began to see that the aim of our groups was love—nothing more. The Lord himself lifted a weight of anxiety about organization from our prayer group. We began to work harder at becoming brothers and sisters than at developing elaborate charts of meetings and systems of pastoral care.

We did not dissolve the structures; we subordinated them to God's purpose. We looked for ways of designing our meetings to allow the growth of loving relationships among us. We encouraged one another to gather together informally for social events. The result was that the group began to become a brotherhood instead of a highly organized but sterile association. People in the group began to be at peace. This assured me that order was coming into proper balance with love.

In the year following our decision to make love our aim, we learned a simple truth which brought us nearer the goal. We began to call each other to use Philippians 2:1-11 as a criterion for governing our personal lives and relationships:

> So if there is any encouragement in Christ, any incentive of love, any participation in the Spirit, any affection and sympathy, complete my joy by being of the same mind,

> having the same love, being in full accord and of one mind. Do nothing from selfishness or conceit, but in humility count others better than yourselves. Let each of you look not only to his own interests, but also to the interests of others. Have this mind among yourselves, which you have in Christ Jesus, who, though he was in the form of God, did not count equality with God a thing to be grasped, but emptied himself, taking the form of a servant, being born in the likeness of men. And being found in human form he humbled himself and became obedient unto death, even death on a cross. Therefore God has highly exalted him and bestowed on him the name which is above every name, that at the name of Jesus every knee should bow, in heaven and on earth and under the earth, and every tongue confess that Jesus Christ is Lord, to the glory of God the Father.

We began to share our hearts' desire to serve the Lord and this desire started to govern our lives. When we faced decisions about our time and money, we asked ourselves whether we were using them with the interests of our brothers and sisters in mind. For example, young men and women who would normally be spending their weekends at the beach chose instead to do house repairs, clean, cook, and care for the children in families where someone was ill. We stopped spending extra money to satisfy selfish desires and began to use it for the needs of others. We took Jesus for our model and became servants.

The Lord loved us with an extraordinary love, a love strong as death. By his Holy Spirit he set our hearts aflame with the same love and he commands us to use it. God's gentle, relentless thrust among us today is the restoration of brotherhood. We should respond with a love strong as death:

> Set me as a seal upon your heart,
> as a seal upon your arm;
> for love is strong as death,
> jealousy is cruel as the grave.
> Its flashes are flashes of fire,
> a most vehement flame.
> Many waters cannot quench love,
> neither can floods drown it.
>
> (Song of Solomon 8:6-7)

The five principles for building with the Lord we have studied here were not arranged as chronological steps that begin with letting Jesus lead and end with love. While building brotherhood has a certain primacy, we must learn to build with all of these principles simultaneously, just as the carpenter learns to use a number of rules as he works. When we are beginning to act as leaders in prayer groups, we are like apprentices. We must begin to employ these spiritual principles, and we will apply some better than others. By the Lord's grace we will learn to use them all well.

Leaders will also learn to use other principles for building with the Lord, for this chapter is only an introduction to a way of forming people into effective Christian groups. There are many principles and these are but five of the most important: letting Jesus lead; trusting the Lord to act; proclaiming Jesus as our ideal; patterning our groups wisely; and learning to love one another as Jesus loved.

2

Developing Leaders Teams

For centuries it has been a common practice in the church and in Christian groups to draw a firm line between the leaders and those being led. The leaders were the clergy who presided and had something to give. The followers were the laymen who sat "in the audience" and came to receive. In the past decade there has been widespread change, recognizing the leadership which all members of the body of Christ not only may, but are bound to exercise by virtue of their initiation into the church. All Christians have a God-given service to perform which is essential to the proper functioning of the local church. "As each has received a gift," instructed Peter, "employ it for one another, as good stewards of God's varied grace: whoever speaks, as one who utters oracles of God; whoever renders service, as one who renders it by the strength which God supplies; in order that in everything God may be glorified through Jesus Christ" (1 Peter 4:10-11).

The key to the revolution which is occurring in Christianity as laymen begin to exercise more leadership has been a renewed understanding of the nature of Christian leadership. Unlike the secular models of leadership—autocrats and business magnates who run organizations to their own advantage—the Christian leader, like Jesus, is the supreme servant. Spiritual leadership is *service*, and we can be called "leaders" because we have a unique service of our own which our brothers and sisters need. This truth is being rediscovered in the church at large, in such developments as the reestablishment of the permanent diaconate among Roman Catholics. However, I think the understanding of leadership as service is being most successfully restored in the prayer groups of the charismatic renewal. Eagerness to serve, faithfulness, and willingness to take responsibility for work characterize prayer group members everywhere. A desire to "serve" in this sense seems to be a common effect of the Pentecostal experience.

While all members of prayer groups usually regard themselves as servants, they have also come to see the importance of recognizing certain individuals as having an overall responsibility for the group. Pastoral teams, service committees, coordinators groups—by whatever name they are called—leaders teams have been organized throughout the charismatic renewal. Except for the action of the Holy Spirit, leaders teams help explain the extraordinary growth and health of the movement more than any single factor.

Why a Team of Leaders?

A team of leaders with overall responsibility for the group will help assure that the group is healthy. Leadership of a group requires a variety of gifts; rarely does one leader, even a very gifted one, possess them all. Among these various gifts are: the ability to sense the Lord's guiding vision for the prayer group; the ability to discern what the prayer group needs in such areas as the prayer meeting and the Life in the Spirit Seminars; the ability to speak in a way which moves the group forward; and the wisdom to organize the group properly. All of these gifts and many others must function interdependently if the prayer group is to be working properly.

Building a leaders team of people with different gifts conforms to the scriptural pattern for the body of Christ. "Now there are varieties of gifts," wrote Paul to the Corinthians, "but the same Spirit . . . To each is given the manifestation of the Spirit for the common good . . . All these gifts are inspired by one and the same Spirit, who apportions to each one individually as he wills . . . For the body does not consist of one member but of many . . . If the whole body were an eye, where would be the hearing? If the whole body were an ear, where would be the sense of smell? But as it is, God arranged the organs in the body, each one of them as he chose. If all were a single organ where would the body be?" (1 Cor. 12:4, 7, 11, 14, 17-19).

The members of a properly functioning leaders team learn how to use their gifts in a way which enables the others to use their gifts most effectively. For example, in one group I worked in, one man with a gift for administration supervised all the routine business and arrangements so that another man could develop his gift of teaching and a third could be free to help others grow in spiritual gifts and service. This does not mean that all the group's leadership activities should be compartmentalized—that a person who gives teaching will never be asked to keep records or to work out schedules. It means only that leaders need to complement each others' gifts, and that leaders should define areas of responsibility with some attention to the abilities of the people involved.

While a team of leaders assures that a variety of gifts will be made available to the group, a team is also a protection from the danger of one-man or one-woman rule. Experience in the charismatic renewal has shown that strong leaders who do not share responsibility and authority with other leaders tend to make mistakes and to get into personal difficulties. A natural leader is often endowed with an independent spirit and a hefty portion of self-righteousness which must be broken through submission to brothers and sisters. Otherwise he will tend to mistake his own will for God's will and attempt to impose it on the prayer group. The team protects the strong leader from the consequences of his dominant tendencies and it protects the prayer group from the problems of his one-man leadership.

I know this situation from the inside—I have many of the

good and bad tendencies of the strong leader. Yet in every prayer group that I have worked with the Lord has joined me to a group of leaders who expected me to yield to the guidance the Lord was giving the whole team. I remember times in the past seven years when I grew angry because a decision in the leaders group did not go my way, decided to support the team's decision, and discovered in the end that the team was right and I had been wrong. One of these occasions involved the very nature of the Grand Haven prayer group. I was sure the Lord wanted the Grand Haven prayer group to become more of a community. However, the other four leaders on the team were just as sure that the Lord was not leading us in that direction. At one point in a particular meeting I threatened to quit if the group did not go the way I thought was right. By the time we gathered for a follow-up meeting I acknowledged that I had been wrong and accepted the vision of the whole team. I saw that the Lord desired to speak through the entire group; the others were correct and I was wrong. My readiness to do this has grown ever since, because I have seen how the Lord desires to speak through the whole group.

The Authority of the Leaders Team

In order to perform their service effectively, leaders teams must have a clearly defined authority over the prayer group's shared activities. The leaders team should exercise authority over all the prayer group's meetings, services, or ministries. It should also take responsibility for related concerns such as maintaining good communications with local churches, helping prayer group members find their service, and building small sharing groups. The leaders team exercises its authority by determining policy, by creating guidelines, by teaching the prayer group a basic pattern of order, by training individuals in their service, by correcting situations or individuals who are out of order, and by making changes in leadership or structure.

Good order requires that the limits of the leaders team's authority be clearly stated and accepted by the prayer group. Normally, the team's authority extends only to whatever the prayer group has or does together and does not include the personal lives of members. The reason for this limit is that in most prayer groups members do not (and should not) commit their whole lives to one another under the authority of the leaders. The leaders team has authority over what an individual does in the prayer meeting, but has no authority over what he does in his own home.

This limitation does not prevent leaders teams from giving brotherly correction when necessary. Frequently, individuals who must be corrected in some prayer group activity also should be corrected in other areas of their lives. Leaders should gently and straightforwardly admonish prayer group members for personal wrongdoing as they would any Christian brother or sister. They cannot *require* individuals to make changes in their personal lives. However, when an individual's wrongdoing or disorder causes disruption in the prayer group, the leaders must take corrective action. In such cases, the leaders have the authority to require changed behavior in meetings, services, or other shared activities.

In some cases, leaders teams do acquire some authority over personal lives. This happens when prayer groups evolve into communities in which people make commitments of their lives to one another. When prayer groups make commitments involving their personal lives, the leaders teams must begin exercising authority over personal lives. Occasionally, an entire prayer group decides to make a community commitment. When such a development occurs, it is necessary to redefine the limits of the leaders team's authority to include personal lives. Or, if the leaders team and some (but not all) of the members of a prayer group decide to enter into a more committed relationship, they must define their new commitments and the authority of the team over them. They must also communicate these decisions to other members of the prayer group who have not entered into the community relationship.

Leaders teams may also have to exercise authority over personal lives when prayer group members decide to live together in extended family households or other living groups of single men or women. The impulse to form such households usually comes from participation in the prayer group. Often members of the leaders team are the first to establish "households." Good order requires the leaders team to have authority over such common living situations when they are formed in the name of the prayer group. Authority in such cases must extend to the personal lives of the people involved, because it is impossible for people to live together without sharing their personal lives with each other. Leaders teams should not allow members to form communal living situations in the name of the prayer group unless they are willing and able to exercise authority over the lives of the individuals in these households.

The exercise of authority in prayer groups must be patterned according to Christian principles. Leaders teams must not acquire a special status or "lord" it over the prayer group. Leaders are servants, and the authority they exercise over the group's life is an authority based upon service. Wise Christian leadership requires close and regular contact with those being served. Effective leaders teams exercise authority well because they are committed to love the individual members of the prayer group and to listen to them seriously.

The Responsibilities of the Leaders Team

The responsibilities of leaders teams vary according to the nature of the prayer groups they serve, but there are some common areas of concern. Leaders teams oversee the group's shared activities. They bring to life its essential elements, make decisions for the prayer group, and take a concern for relationships within and outside the group.

The leaders team takes concern for what happens at the group's meetings and in its courses such as the Life in the Spirit Seminars. "Taking a concern" means that the leaders see that everything happens in the right way. If something goes wrong, the leaders must act to correct it. This does not mean that the leaders *do* everything; rather, they function as managers who *enable* others to do their service well. For example, if the leaders team sees that many people completing Life in the Spirit Seminars drift away from the group, they would study the situation and find ways of helping the entire group to correct it. This was our approach in Grand Haven when the leaders team noticed that seminar discussion leaders did not seem to be as helpful to people as they should be. The members of the leaders team did not decide to lead all discussions themselves but instead provided the discussion leaders with a better understanding of their role and with training in praying for people. The leaders do not *do* everything, but instead make sure that people in the group perform their services properly.

If something is missing in the life of a prayer group, the leaders team is responsible for searching out ways of supplying it. For example, when there is hardly any prophecy in meetings for a long period of time, the team needs to restore the free exercise of this spiritual gift. The whole prayer group must pray, expecting the Lord to act. The leaders must teach about prophecy, encourage people to speak out, and help people overcome their fears and shyness. They should speak a supportive word to a person who stumbles through a prophecy and encourage him to go ahead and use the gift. The leaders should also form a group of people who have yielded to prophecy regularly to pray and learn more about the gift. The Lord honors such active faith with results.

Prayer groups are faced with a multitude of decisions ranging from very important questions such as how to lead new people to be baptized in the Holy Spirit to routine matters such as how much coffee to prepare for refreshments. The leaders team is the place where the buck stops for all decisions. It will certainly delegate the authority and responsibility for many decisions to other members of the group. But a wise leaders team will set down a guiding policy for each area delegated, keep in close contact with it, and reserve the important decisions to itself.

The Grand Haven leaders followed this policy after they formed a special team to be responsible for a prayer room after the weekly meeting where people with special needs received prayer with laying on of hands. We had confidence in the team and knew they would do a good job. But we also made sure that we were in regular contact with the team and knew what was going on. We knew that many important things happened to people in prayer rooms, so we were careful. We worked out policy with the prayer room team. We decided that the team would meet to pray beforehand; that it would not pray for the baptism in the Holy Spirit and other things. When new questions came up, the leaders team consulted the prayer room team and then decided how to proceed. For example, the leaders team decided that the prayer room team should not pray for deliverance from evil spirits.

Leaders teams have a responsibility to help the prayer group develop sound Christian personal relationships. The Lord wants prayer groups to train us in the practice of Christian love. Thus the team should design the activities of the prayer group to allow as many opportunities as possible for people to develop friendships and brotherly relationships. When disagreements or other problems that affect the prayer group's common activities erupt, the leaders team has a responsibility to help all the individuals involved resolve their differences. They must correct the situation in order to assure that the prayer group may continue to conduct its life peacefully.

The quality of relationships among prayer group members is directly connected to the quality of relationships among those on the leaders team. If the leaders seriously wish the prayer group to be one, they should begin with themselves. When the leaders team is torn apart with bad relationships, that condition will project itself into the prayer group. The place, then, to begin building brotherhood is with the leaders. The leaders should frequently discuss the quality of their relationships. They should grow in their willingness and ability to submit to the Lord and to each other.

The leaders team is also responsible for good relations with the local secular society and the local churches and dioceses. For example, when the prayer group uses public or church buildings, the leaders team should see to it that everyone treats the property with respect and that those charged with cleaning up do their job well. The leaders team should also be sure that the prayer group is reliable financially. All bills should be paid on time and no debts incurred which cannot be paid.

If prayer groups are to cooperate with the Lord in his work, they must relate correctly to local churches. Leaders should consider these relationships as one of their most serious obligations. The concluding chapter presents some advice on how leaders can conduct these relationships properly.

The Team At Work

There are a few principles of organization which leaders teams can use to prevent confusion in relationships and to assure that they are faithfully doing their jobs. These principles involve headship of the team, an orderly procedure for structuring meetings, and agreements about how the team will make decisions.

Leaders should designate someone as the head of the team. I have participated in leaders meetings where all behaved as the head, and, as a result, we accomplished nothing. The head is not a dictator, although he does exercise authority when necessary. His task is to facilitate the work of the team. During meetings, he moves the group through its agenda, conducts discussions, brings the leaders team to decisions, and holds it to agreements. With a recognized head, the leaders team can perform its work in good order. Without a head, the team is in danger of succumbing to competition, disorder, and unnecessary disagreement.

Leaders teams should structure their meetings so that they can care for all their responsibilities in an orderly way. They should use agendas for their meetings and designate meetings for specific purposes. The Grand Haven team used to meet for one-and-a-half hours each week. A portion of each meeting was set aside for a review of some essential area: one week we evaluated the prayer meetings; the next week we planned teaching; the third week we reviewed the Life in the Spirit Seminars; at the fourth meeting of the month we evaluated the prayer group's other gatherings and planned for them. Having a definite pattern for considering these areas helped us to be responsible and minimized the chance of neglect.

Leaders teams should agree on the way they are going to come to a decision. If they do not agree in advance about the decision-making process, discussion will wander and their work will bog down in confusion. The norm for decisions about all important matters coming before the leaders team should be consensus; the group will talk a matter through until everyone agrees on a decision or solution. Decision-making by consensus requires a high degree of forbearance and an eagerness to submit on the part of all the leaders. No one person should hold up a decision by consensus except for the most serious reasons. Decision-making by consensus works only when the leaders are committed to being brothers and sisters in the Lord. When this brotherhood does not exist, no procedure for making decisions will prevent division and controversy.

Who Should Be On Leaders Teams?

The guidance of the Holy Spirit is essential in choosing leaders to have overall responsibility for prayer groups. His leadings assure us of finding the individuals who can serve us best. The Lord has also provided us with criteria to aid us in identifying the people who should be our leaders. All members of prayer groups should understand these criteria so that they will be able to identify and support good leaders.

Several New Testament lists of characteristics for the "overseers" of Christian assemblies apply to prayer group leaders. The most important lists are found in 1 Tim. 3:1-3 and Titus 1:5-9. According to St. Paul, the marks of a Christian leader include the following:

—above reproach (of impeccable character, of unquestionable integrity)

—not arrogant (not self-willed, not presumptuous)

—not quick-tempered (not quarrelsome)

—not a drunkard (not a heavy drinker)

—not violent (not pugnacious, not hot-tempered)

—not greedy for gain (not out to make money, not grasping)

—hospitable (a friend to those he does not know)

—a lover of goodness

—sensible (soberminded, discreet, master of himself)

—a man of prayer (holy)

—self-controlled (temperate)

—a capable teacher

—able to manage his own household well

—not a recent convert

—well thought of by outsiders

There are four questions in particular which members of prayer groups should ask about individuals who are under consideration for overall leadership: 1) Is the person bringing his personal life and relationships into good order? 2) Is he free of major psychological and emotional problems? 3) Does he have the appropriate gifts? 4) Is the prospective leader fully committed to the prayer group?

People who will have responsibility over our groups must be people who are bringing every area of their own lives into right order. Members of leaders teams should be learning to sort out their priorities and commitments so that they have time for essentials such as personal prayer, sleep, time with their families, and physical exercise. They should be able to manage their own personal affairs well, especially their finances.

Husbands and fathers should be well on the way to building proper Christian relationships in their families. They should be actively leading and caring for their wives and children. Wives should be learning how to help their husbands in forming the family. Single people, both young and old, and priests and sisters must also be in right relationships, especially in their living situations. A young person who is rebellious at home or a sister who cannot get along with others at her convent cannot be counted on to lead our prayer groups. People who are in bad relationships at home inevitably carry their problems into their personal relationships in the prayer group.

When applying this criterion, we should be careful about too rigidly expecting perfection. Candidates for leadership need not be candidates for canonization. However, they must at least be well along the way to getting their lives and relationships into right order.

Secondly, when choosing leaders, prayer groups should determine whether candidates are free of serious psychological and emotional problems. This prohibition applies to those with *serious* difficulties; it does not disqualify someone who is occasionally plagued by anxiety, depression, or other emotional disturbance. Hardly anyone raised in the modern world is free from all emotional difficulty. However, those with major emotional or psychological problems should under no circumstances be in a position of leadership in a prayer group. Placing such individuals on the leaders team would be an injustice to them and a disservice to the prayer group. Making such a person a leader is unfair and wrong because someone who is incapable of being responsible even in small things will be harmed by the grave responsibilities of leadership. It is also obvious that it is a disservice to the prayer group to expect a needy, irresponsible person to care for its needs responsibly. It is sometimes difficult to recognize a serious emotional disturbance in a prospective leader. However, two factors usually identify such people: they are unreliable in tasks they are given to do, and their relationships with other people—particularly those closest to them—are in a state of chronic disorder.

Prayer groups should take this advice seriously. Unfortunately, people with serious psychological problems often seek leadership positions in charismatic groups as a way of making up for their failures in other situations. Frequently they manifest some charism and appear to be very "spiritual." They claim that their spiritual gifts demonstrate that they are called to lead. Such people may have genuine charisms and they may be authentically spiritual. However, as long as they have unresolved major psychological disorders, they are not called to be on the leaders team. Because it is not always easy to recognize people with serious psychological problems, prayer groups should proceed with faith and courage to be sure that people with serious problems do not become prayer group leaders.

A third criterion for identifying leaders is: "Does this person have the spiritual gifts necessary to be a leader?" Each person placed on the leaders team should have some spiritual gift which qualifies him to bear responsibility. Members of the team should be used by the Lord for prophecy, teaching, and exhortation. Some should be good at overseeing the whole group. Some should have a gift for organizing and administering. All team members will not have all the gifts, but the team as a whole should have most if not all of them. When applying this criterion, prayer groups should ask themselves if the Lord seems to be using the person under consideration in ways which equip him to take an overall concern for the group. This principle applies to all areas of service, not just to selecting leaders. For example, a group looking for someone to give explanation talks to newcomers would seek an individual who already shows gifts of evangelism.

A fourth criterion is summed up in the question: "Is the prospective leader fully committed to the group?" No matter how gifted a prospective leader may be, he cannot properly care for the group if he is only a casual participant who comes to gatherings when he has nothing else to do. The leaders team must be able to attend all the prayer group's meetings and the team meetings as well. People who have many duties in other movements and organizations ought not be on the leaders team until they sort out their commitments and make the prayer group a priority. This is true too for priests and nuns who are heavily involved in church activities: they cannot effectively lead prayer groups if they are not participating fully in the group's activities. Gifted people who have little contact with the group can serve as advisers, but they should not have overall responsibility for the prayer group.

Two further considerations, while they are not strictly criteria for leaders, help determine the composition of the leaders team. These are the roles of married women and young people.

In my experience, married women serve best as members of the overall leaders team when their husbands are also members of the team. Normally the wife, no matter how well qualified, should not be on the leaders team when her husband is not a leader. When a couple is on a leaders team, both husband and wife should meet the criteria for membership on the team independently; neither should be placed in leadership merely because his spouse qualifies for service on the team. In the interest of good order in the family, a wife should not be on the leaders team when her leadership in the prayer group may be an obstacle to her husband's leadership at home or an obstacle to performing her duties as wife and mother. Also for the sake of family order, wives whose husbands are not involved in the prayer group should not be on the team. This does not mean that women have no service if their husbands are not active in the group or are not leaders. It means only that such women should not have responsibility to oversee the whole prayer group. These married women can perform valuable service in other prayer group activities, such as exercising spiritual gifts in the prayer meeting, working in the book ministry, or serving in the prayer room.

Young people in their late teens and early 20's are exercising leadership in some prayer groups and are doing excellent work. Their youthfulness brings a zest and life to many groups, but their very youthfulness requires special concern to assure the effectiveness of their leadership. Precisely because young people are young, they are still working out major decisions in their lives. Questions such as vocation, marriage, school, and occupation can dominate them, unsettle them, and make it difficult for them to bear the responsibility of overall leadership. For this reason, young leaders should be working closely with more mature leaders who can assure their stability. For example, one would normally expect that a young single person with major life decisions still before him ought not to be the head of the leaders team. In prayer groups where the right relationship exists, young people are able to lead prayer groups effectively.

How to Build a Leaders Team

Leaders teams are formed in a variety of ways. Many have evolved naturally out of the early experience of prayer groups: the people who were the hosts of early house prayer meetings assume some kind of pastoral care. Sometimes a few people who have been exercising informal leadership begin to take more responsibility for the prayer group's activities. In some cases, a very strong leader will gather a team together. In all these situations, the prayer group does not take the initiative in constituting the leaders team. Rather the leaders team comes together on its own—gradually or at some specific time—and the prayer group tacitly or explicitly accepts its leadership. These are appropriate and legitimate ways for leaders teams to develop.

In other cases, prayer groups take more initiative in starting leaders teams. The advice that follows is mainly concerned with these situations. I do not mean to unsettle prayer groups that never went through a selective process to create the original leaders group. The advice in this section should not undermine prayer group members' support for established teams. In fact, if prayer groups apply this advice properly to regroup teams and add new members, they can strengthen their leadership.

The guidelines presented here are designed to help prayer

groups which are about to set up leaders teams. Groups which are about to make some change in their leadership structure can profitably adapt them to their needs.

First, prayer groups should take some time together to discuss important questions such as direction for the group and leadership. Prayer meetings ought not to become discussion groups, but prayer groups should gather occasionally to talk about matters of common concern. Only the "superspiritual" would make the mistake of avoiding all discussion and resolving issues exclusively through the discernment of prayer. Prayer is certainly an important part of setting up a leaders team but it does not eliminate the basic human need to talk together.

Second, prayer groups should have some teaching about leaders teams, their authority and responsibilities, and the proper criteria for membership on the team. Instruction about leaders teams will form the prayer group in a way which will allow members to make intelligent decisions in response to the leadings of the Holy Spirit. Understanding the right criteria for membership, for example, will help members avoid choosing people for typically mistaken reasons, such as "Harry hasn't missed a prayer meeting for five years and deserves some recognition." If no one in the group is able to develop a presentation on the subject, the prayer group might decide to read this chapter and discuss it.

Third, in order to proceed peacefully, the prayer groups should have a clearly stated method worked out for appointing the leaders team. Prayer groups have used a number of different ways with success. The procedure I recommend, and which I have seen used successfully in several groups, involves teaching, listening, and choosing. After teaching and several weeks of listening to the Lord, members gather and prepare a list of those people who meet the criteria. Individuals are asked to list only those persons to whom they would want to entrust the direction and care of the group. The prayer group determines in advance how large the team should be and how many times a person must be named on the lists in order to become a member of the team. Like all processes, this one is open to abuse if participants behave more politically than spiritually in its execution.

When prayer groups decide to establish a leaders team, there often arises a question about the position of people who have been exercising an informal leadership in the group. These persons may very well be the right people to constitute a leaders team, but they should not automatically join it. Those providing informal leadership may not be able to serve well on the leaders team. While we should not be hasty in deciding that a person who has been leading informally should not be on the team, neither should we place him in leadership if he fails to meet the criteria. We should always remain open to changes in overall leadership.

Making initial appointments to the leaders team temporary and subject to evaluation creates a healthy flexibility. For example, one prayer group adds new members to the overall leaders team for a period of one year. During that time the other leaders and the prayer group determine if the person is able to perform his service well. At the end of the year a decision is reached about whether he should continue as a permanent member of the team or be encouraged to work in some other service. This practice provides an effective way to make necessary changes in leadership and to help people find the right service. Undoing a mistaken appointment to the leaders team is very difficult when it has not been clear from the beginning that the appointment was temporary and subject to evaluation. When a person leaves a leaders team, the decision should be explained to the prayer group gently and in a way which protects his self-respect.

In some way, the members of the prayer group must express their support for the team. This is vital both when the leaders team evolves naturally and presents itself to the prayer group, and when it develops through a selective process determined and executed by the prayer group. For example, in Grand Haven when we moved from an informal team of couples to a pastoral team of five leaders, all the regular participants were asked to recognize the team and follow its direction over the group's activities. The leaders explained the changes in membership and in the structure of the team; the prayer group responded and indicated their acceptance by praying for the new team.

The best method for recognizing a leaders team is the formulation of a simple agreement which specifies the authority of the team, the members, and any other details such as term of office. All should understand that the agreement is serious but that it is not permanent. The prayer group could revise its decisions later if need occurred to do so. After teaching and discussion, the prayer group can be asked to assent to the agreement in some way. For example, each person could state publicly his willingness to accept the leaders team and to accept its authority as specified in the agreement. Prayer groups should set their leaders teams free to lead by publicly acknowledging their authority and responsibility.

Keeping the Whole in View

To summarize this chapter, I would like to add a sixth principle for building with the Lord to the five discussed in the preceding chapter. The prayer group is God's gift to us and leaders teams are good stewards of this gift. The leaders' responsibility extends from large matters—such as following the Lord—to small matters such as book displays. To do their job well the leaders must learn how to keep the whole prayer group in view. Viewing groups as a whole is a capacity which is not natural to many and therefore we must learn how to do it.

The ability to care for groups as a whole is related to the spiritual gift which Paul had in mind when he listed "pastor" among the gifts of Christ for his church (Eph. 4:11). Reflecting on the role of "pastor" can teach us about what it means to keep the whole in view. A "pastor" is a shepherd. He knows and cares for every sheep in the fold, but he does not tend the flock one by one but as a unit. He moves the whole flock from one place to another. He takes a concern that all have food and water. He makes sure that each sheep has the best natural protection from enemies. He plans ahead so that he is assured of being able to care for the flock tomorrow. He knows the land and the roads so he can lead the flock in safety. The "pastor" puts himself in a position which allows him to keep his eye on the whole flock. Leaders teams must take the same position in regard to the activities of the prayer group. No element of the group's life together should be outside the team's vision.

Leaders teams can learn to keep the whole in view only by doing it. It can begin by having a prayerful discussion about the prayer group. Questions such as the following will help bring the whole into focus: How did the group come together? What service does the group provide for its members and for the local area? What purpose has the Lord assigned it and what is he calling it to? What are the activities of the prayer group? Is the leaders team in contact with every element of the prayer group's life? How can the leaders team give better care to every common activity? What does the prayer group need to hear at this point in order to follow the Lord more faithfully? Are the leaders themselves growing in love and brotherhood? Have they paid sufficient attention to their working relationships? Effective leaders teams regularly devote a significant amount of time to consider questions of this kind.

Leaders teams should look for opportunities to put this principle into practice. Using agendas and allocating time to discuss important areas regularly are ways of keeping the whole in view. Planning and evaluation are also ways leaders can keep the whole in view. Planning well in advance for major changes such as adopting a new kind of leaders group or starting a second meeting for regular members has the effect of requiring the leaders team to step back and see the whole of what the Lord is doing with the prayer group. Spending time planning smaller events such as the content of an important prayer meeting teaching has a similar effect.

Engaging in a process of evaluation will also assist leaders in seeing the prayer group as a whole. Leaders teams should evaluate regular activities including the weekly prayer meeting to see how well the prayer group is responding to the Lord. Evaluation is an especially important part of the process of making changes in the prayer group.

A positive evaluation can confirm the change and a negative one may help us correct a mistake. Some might fear that planning and evaluation are "unspiritual" and inappropriate for prayer groups. To the contrary, they are intelligent processes which can conform to the leadings of the Holy Spirit. Both are valuable operations for leaders teams and should become a normal part of their activities.

Keeping the whole in view is an essential principle for building Christian groups well. It assures us of being responsible stewards and it enables us to move the whole group in response to the leadings of the Holy Spirit.

3

Bringing Prayer Meetings to Life

The prayer meeting is the heart of the prayer group. Without it, most prayer groups would never have formed, for prayer groups are associations which grow out of prayer meetings and are sustained by them. The prayer meeting is a gathering of people who assemble to praise the Lord, to listen to him, and to grow in loving one another. They express their praise in a wide variety of ways: song, prayer, silence, and sometimes even with applause and shouts. The Lord speaks to the assembly through Scripture, teaching, exhortation, charismatic gifts, and sharing. Before, during, and after the gathering, participants grow in learning to love one another with supportive words and expressions of affection.

The prayer meeting is the heart of the prayer group because it centers the participants on the Lord. Loving the Lord with our whole heart, our whole mind, with our spirit, with our body, and all our possessions is the first requirement of God. In the prayer meeting, loving the Lord wholeheartedly is the essential activity which we express in diverse ways. Praise and song not only draw us nearer to him, but enable the Lord to draw us nearer to each other. In the prayer meeting the Lord provides us with a lesson in brotherhood which we can apply in our daily lives. Thus the prayer meeting also prepares us to follow the Lord's second great commandment which is essential to the Christian life—loving one another.

Taking Responsibility for Meetings

Neither human ingenuity nor group dynamics can account for the wholesome effect prayer meetings have on participants. The Spirit of the Lord governs and inspires each prayer meeting. No two are ever alike, for the Lord meets us where we are and desires us to express our praise in different ways. The Lord's word to us unfolds according to our needs and according to his plan for us. The Holy Spirit inspires the songs, prompts the exhortations and sharings, creates moments of silence or loud praise, suggests a Scripture passage or speaks through the gift of prophecy. He coordinates the various elements into a unity which is so striking that newcomers often comment on how much effort must go into developing the themes of the meeting.

Because a prayer meeting is inspired by the Lord, some participants feel that to attempt to do anything to direct it or change it is "unspiritual." To the contrary, to refrain from taking action to build the prayer meeting is itself a dangerous unbiblical approach. Paul's teaching to the Corinthians corrected their unspiritual use of the charisms and showed them how to improve their meetings:

> What then, brethren? When you come together, each one has a hymn, a lesson, a revelation, a tongue, or an interpretation. Let all things be done for edification. If any speak in a tongue, let there be only two or at most three, and each in turn; and let one interpret. But if there is no one to interpret, let each of them keep silence in church and speak to himself and to God. Let two or three prophets speak, and let the others weigh what is said. If a revelation is made to another sitting by, let the first be silent. For you can all prophesy one by one, so that all may learn and all be encouraged; and the spirits of prophets are subject to prophets. For God is not a God of confusion but of peace. (1 Cor. 14:26-33)

While the Lord does not want us to manipulate the elements of our prayer meetings, he expects us to work with him in developing them. The Lord wants each person to prepare himself for the prayer meeting by cultivating his receptivity to God's word and by seeking to participate actively and fully in the meeting. Further, he has taught us extensively about the importance of having leadership and order for prayer meetings. We can take steps to encourage the development of forms of praise and to bring to life elements which might be weak or lacking.

Preparing Ourselves

Every participant has a responsibility for the prayer meeting. Our openness to the Holy Spirit releases the power which the Lord makes available for our benefit. Our readiness to cooperate with the Lord enables the Holy Spirit to serve us in the gathering. An assembly of people whose hearts are not prepared will not experience very much of God's action; neither will individuals who sit passively in a prayer meeting. Each person attending the prayer meeting must cultivate the right attitudes of heart beforehand.

To cultivate right attitudes, we must renounce wrong approaches. Many people approach a prayer meeting as though it were a spiritual filling station which satisfies their personal spiritual needs. This approach reflects both a wrong attitude toward prayer meetings and a faulty understanding of Christian life. People who come to prayer meetings solely to seek "ministry" are often so full of self-concern that they are unable to serve the needs of others. If everyone attended the prayer meeting only to have his needs met, the prayer meeting would not function well because there would be no one to give. Everyone would be draining off life without giving of himself.

Beneath this selfish approach to prayer meetings is an inadequate conception of Christian life. Our lives are not meant to be a routine of defeat and drudgery in which we confront problem after problem. People who look to prayer meetings as an escape from the monotonous slavery of their lives need rather to look to Jesus so that he might set them free. The Lord, by his death and resurrection, has conquered Satan, sin, death, and disease. He has made us his partners in applying this victory. Our daily lives are not free of problems, but we can live our lives joyfully, standing with Jesus and peacefully battling in the war already won. If we are full of self-concern and live a problem-centered life, we need to repent and begin living a life centered on Jesus and filled with service to others. When participants are living a victorious Christian life, they can come to the prayer meeting with their hearts prepared to serve others. A prayer meeting that honors the Lord and builds brotherhood is one in which participants do not seek to fill their own needs but eagerly fulfill the needs of others.

Faithfulness to our daily time of prayer and Scripture study is an essential part of our preparation for the prayer meeting. We cannot expect to participate properly if we restrict our prayer to corporate worship on Sunday morning and the Wednesday evening prayer meeting. Coming before the Lord daily to pray and reflect upon his word is essential—not optional—to the Christian life. When participants are faithful in daily private prayer, prayer meetings come alive, because the people who come together have maintained a lively individual contact with the Lord.

Praying for the prayer meeting should be one specific focus of our daily prayer. We should pray for all the participants, especially for those who will be coming for the first time. We should ask the Lord what he wants to say at the gathering and what we can do to bring out his message. (Sometimes the Lord uses our times of private prayer to begin to inspire a prophetic word for the prayer meeting or to suggest a text which he wants read to the assembly.) During our daily prayer we should renounce self-concern and seek ways of serving others at the prayer meeting. We should ask the Lord to show us how we can care for brothers and sisters at the prayer meeting. We should also pray for the Lord to pour out his spiritual gifts on the prayer meeting and in particular that he guide the prayer meeting leader.

We should spend time each week reflecting on what the Lord said and did at the previous week's prayer meeting. Anticipation and eagerness to hear the Lord are right attitudes of heart for us to cultivate. Training ourselves to listen to the Lord during our private prayer will prepare us to listen to him at the gathering. But listening is not enough. After we hear the Lord, we need to *do* what he tells us. The Word of God is not idle and unproductive; he wants to stir us to act. A practice which helps us pay attention to the Lord is to regularly discuss the prayer meeting afterwards with our families and with others who attended. When all participants are listening, hearing, and obeying the Lord, the prayer meeting works as a source of direction for our Christian lives.

Establishing Good Order

Bringing order into a prayer meeting means deciding in advance on certain basic patterns of order so that the gathering is free to devote itself to the Lord in prayer. Having a definite time to start and stop, agreeing not to have sharing until after a certain point, appointing a prayer meeting leader, and having an explanation room before or after the gathering are examples of helpful patterns. Our action to structure the prayer meeting does not replace the action of the Holy Spirit, but rather gives his action greater scope.

The appointment of a prayer meeting leader is the single most important element in establishing good order. Prayer meetings which have no recognized leaders have a difficult time following Jesus. They are vulnerable to disunity, competition, deadness, and other problems, and are easily disrupted by disturbances. Leaderless prayer meetings are not only unpractical, but they are also unbiblical. The Lord's pattern for his church and Christian groups within it is clearly that we be submitted to leaders in all things, including worship.

A good prayer meeting leader does more than start and stop the meeting. He centers the group on Jesus with exhortation. He redirects the meeting should it begin to drift. He stirs up praise and spiritual gifts. He keeps the meeting flowing in the Holy Spirit by moving the group from one element to the next. He encourages sharing and teaching. He deals with disturbances should they come up. He draws attention to the Lord's message, and he may even attempt to summarize it at some point during the meeting or at the end.

Led by the Holy Spirit, the prayer meeting leader directs the course of our common prayer. The Lord gives the prayer meeting leader a gift to perceive what he wants to accomplish, inspiring him with an understanding of God's plan for the meeting and even specific leadings for what should happen. The Lord's guidance enables the prayer meeting leader to move the meeting ahead. He senses the Lord's timing for various elements; he may even know which song the Spirit is about to inspire or who is about to prophesy. By the Lord's grace, prayer meeting leaders are able to assist the Lord in building all the elements of the meeting into a unity.

Not every member of the prayer group has the necessary gifts to be a good prayer meeting leader. The leaders team should only appoint those people to whom the Lord has given these gifts. Often, members of the leaders team lead all the prayer meetings, but sometimes a prayer meeting leader will not be on the leaders team. In prayer groups where more than one person has a gift for leading prayer meetings, there is often a system of rotation.

Most prayer groups do not have a developed structure for their meetings in the sense that the various elements of the meeting are not precisely scheduled in a definite order. However, many groups have found that a loose structure is helpful in making the prayer meeting work better. For example, some groups ask that no one stand up and share during the first 45 minutes or so, in order to allow enough time for praise and worship. I have found that this request does not place a limit on the Holy Spirit, but frees him to lead the group into deeper prayer and praise. Another helpful request is to ask people to raise their petitions to the Lord at a certain time during the meeting, usually in the last few minutes. Groups which initiated this practice did so because petition had so dominated their style of prayer that there was little opportunity for praise or other forms of worship. Establishing patterns such as these releases the Holy Spirit to produce a variety of gifts and experiences in the prayer meeting.

Many prayer groups have established several auxiliary services as a way of ordering their prayer meetings. An explanation room where newcomers can hear a presentation about the work of the Holy Spirit helps guests participate in the meeting more comfortably. Some groups have prayer rooms after the gathering which enables them to serve people who desire prayer for special intentions. Explanation sessions and prayer rooms order the prayer meeting by simplifying its functions. When participants know they can ask questions at the explanation room or receive prayer afterwards, they do not look to the prayer meeting to meet these needs.

Prayer groups will discover other simple ways to bring more order into their activities. Those which adopt intelligent patterns will benefit, for their prayer meetings will be equipped to follow the design of the Lord more peacefully.

Active Participation

All persons attending a prayer meeting should be active participants. No one should regard himself as a part of an audience or as a passive guest. When the group is praying aloud, all should join in. Even those who are not good singers should blend their voices in when the assembly is singing. We should respond when the Lord seems to be inspiring us to pray aloud, to exercise a spiritual gift such as prophecy, to read a Scripture text, or to share from our experience. We should act on these leadings, believing the Holy Spirit will use them for the benefit of the group. We should work at listening to others when the Lord is giving his message through them.

At root, active participation means maintaining a sense of the Lord's presence throughout the prayer meeting. From the beginning of the gathering, we should center our minds and hearts on Jesus, handing over to him the concerns and problems we have brought with us. The Holy Spirit, the very presence of the Lord in us, will help us maintain our awareness of the Lord as we pray. Should our attention drift, we should call ourselves back to the Lord and what he is doing in the prayer meeting. Simply taking part in all the elements of the gathering keeps us before the Lord and open to his leadings.

We should submit our participation in the prayer meeting to the direction of the leader. If he calls for a period of silence or asks us to stand and praise the Lord aloud, we should quickly follow his direction. Our quick response makes it easier for the prayer meeting leader to perform his service, because it sets him free to lead in a direct, active fashion. Our common submission is a form of active participation; it creates a prayer meeting ready to hear and follow Jesus as one body. Unity among participants releases the power of the Spirit and creates an environment in which he is freer to act in striking ways.

We should fit our contributions into the flow of the meeting which the Holy Spirit is directing. A little experience will teach us how to recognize what activity is appropriate at which point. Most of us will have no difficulty in seeing that interrupting a teaching to exercise the gift of tongues would be out of place. But it is harder to determine whether starting a song or praying aloud is proper during a period of silence. As we grow in the Holy Spirit we will learn to distinguish among different kinds of silence at gatherings. Sometimes silence is "dead" and we should freely pray aloud or start a song if we feel so led. At other times the silence is meant to be profoundly uninterrupted or it is a time of preparation for a very serious word from the Lord. It does not take long for us to learn that a personal sharing would not be appropriate at these times.

Sometimes it is not clear to us how contributions to the meeting relate to the content of other sharings. Context is a helpful guide for our contributions. Normally, our sharing should not be so shockingly different from all the preceding sharings as to jar the assembly into a state of puzzlement. However, the Lord may want to jar us from our complacency with a word that does not relate nicely to everything else that has been said. The direction of the prayer meeting leader is most helpful. If he is active enough in guiding the course of the gathering, people should rarely be uncertain about the appropriateness of their contributions.

Active participation also involves our openness to charismatic gifts such as tongues, interpretation, and prophecy. The Holy Spirit may call upon anyone living in union with him to exercise these spiritual gifts. Charisms are not marks of "super-Christians." They are tools for strengthening Christians assembled in a group, and their use depends upon the Lord's gift rather than any excellence in the person exercising them. We should not block the operation of the Holy Spirit by holding on to the false conviction that we could not possibly prophesy or give an interpretation. In his merciful humor, the Lord often gives these word gifts to people who regard themselves as the most unlikely candidates for them. We should actively break down our reticence and renounce the lies which would prevent us from exercising spiritual gifts. In 1 Corinthians 14, Paul instructed us all to eagerly desire the spiritual gifts which build up the body of Christ.

When a person senses that the Lord desires to speak through him, he should turn to Jesus, tell him that he wants to obey, and watch for the right time to speak. Sometimes we are afraid that we might make a mistake, but mistakes are nothing to fear. The Lord knows our heart's desire to serve him without mistakes. He will speak through our imperfect prophecy and teach us how to exercise the gift without errors. Equipped with faith in Jesus and surrounded by the love of brothers and sisters, we can learn to use the charisms effectively.

Active, sensitive listening is also important for effective prayer meetings. Paying attention to our brothers and sisters is a way of paying attention to the Lord. Supportive eye contact and a smile are ways the Holy Spirit reassures a person that his sharing is worthwhile. Even while we are on our feet speaking, Satan likes to undermine our contributions by telling us that we are doing a terrible job and no one likes it. A nod of approval or agreement can help a person overcome fear and exercise his gift more freely. People who are speaking up for the first time especially need our encouragement. What they need least at that moment is to see the "old timers" bowing their heads, eyes closed, praying furiously. Such behavior can cause them to wonder what is so wrong with their sharing that it has driven people to prayer.

A supportive word after the prayer meeting to someone who has shared or exercised a spiritual gift will help build future gatherings. Our encouragement frequently erases the doubts and second thoughts people often have about their contributions. Many of us have inherited bad self-images from our secular environment. The enemy paralyzes many Christians by exploiting this self-hatred and lack of self-confidence. Brothers and sisters who express their appreciation for someone's faith-building sharing or a prophecy can release people from the crippling bondage of self-doubt. They will be freer to share even more powerfully the next time the Holy Spirit leads them.

Learning to Express Praise

Since the beginning of the charismatic renewal, the Lord has taught prayer groups how to worship him in a great variety of ways. Growth in expressing praise is his gift, but we can take appropriate action to make it easier for him to give it. Leaders must be willing to teach us how to pray together; we must be docile—willing to learn and change.

Leaders teams and prayer meeting leaders play a significant role in preparing groups to grow in expressing praise. Leaders should frequently talk to the prayer group about its forms of prayer, and encourage people to improve. Sometimes leaders are hesitant to teach about praise, thinking that instruction about spiritual activity may somehow destroy its authenticity. For myself, I had to overcome my own reticence, and a little resistance from some others, the first time I instructed the Grand Haven group about how to sing in tongues. I had observed a greater freedom in spiritual song in groups that had received such instruction; this convinced me to speak about it to my group. As a result of the teaching, the Grand Haven prayer meeting learned to sing in the Spirit with greater depth and variety. This has persuaded me that it is not only proper to train people in spiritual activities, but it also unspiritual to refrain from doing so. A truly spiritual approach to Christian life contends with human frailties. One of these frailties is that we need to be taught.

Participants in prayer meetings should cultivate a desire to grow in expressing their praise to the Lord. This willingness to learn allows the Lord to teach us. Early in the Catholic charismatic renewal, we were unwilling to raise our arms in prayer because we regarded such gestures as "cultural baggage" from Pentecostal traditions, alien to our Catholic heritage. As we became more open to learning, Jesus taught us that uplifted hands are an appropriate way of praising him. Scripture, early Christian art, and age-old liturgical practice show us that if raising our hands in prayer is "cultural baggage," it is "cultural baggage" that has persisted for centuries. Our docility opens us to expressions of praise the Spirit wants us to use; our prudence prevents us from thoughtlessly adopting behavior which is unbecoming to a follower of Jesus. We should expect the Lord to make us both docile and discerning.

The prayer meeting leader should frequently use his opening remarks as an opportunity to teach participants. He should endeavor to bring life to every element of the prayer meeting. At one time, he may teach about openness to spiritual gifts or maintaining an awareness of the Lord's presence. At another, he may explain how to join in the flow of the gathering or how to share. Opportunities for teaching present themselves during the meeting. For example, if the group fails to wait for the interpretation of a message in tongues, the prayer meeting leader may decide to give a brief instruction about the operation of these spiritual gifts. When the group sings half-heartedly, he may exhort them to vigor and unity in song.

Exhortation, the word of praise, testimony, and spiritual song are especially helpful in setting a prayer meeting free to praise. Often, prayer meeting leaders open gatherings with an exhortation to center our hearts and minds on the Lord Jesus. Many groups have learned that a single-hearted response to such a call to worship releases praise which spills over into the entire assembly. Exhortation during the gathering is a way of engaging our hearts to express love for the Lord in some particular way. Clear, authoritative exhortation has brought new life to many a dying prayer meeting.

The "word of praise" refers to the time when everyone prays aloud spontaneously in his own words. Some pray in tongues, some in English, some sing softly. The "word of praise" is not an unpleasant cacophony; the Holy Spirit guides many voices in uncanny blends. Words of praise in gatherings resemble the sound of God's creation praising him—the gentle rumbling of mighty waters acknowledging the Lord. Simultaneous spontaneous prayer brings the unity of heart which the Lord uses to deepen the prayer experience of the assembly.

Testimony to the Lord's great deeds in our lives brings out praise by proclaiming his glory. The Holy Spirit leads some to share personal experiences as a way of building faith and strengthening his message for the evening. Some prayer groups invite an individual to come prepared to give a personal testimony. Whether spontaneous or prepared, testimony draws heartfelt praise from the assembly.

Spiritual song releases people to praise the Lord more freely. Music enhances our prayer. It evokes different responses depending upon the leading of the Spirit and the kind of song. Prayer groups soon learn by experience which songs plunge the gathering into quiet worship and which songs of celebration open a time of loud praise. "Singing in the Spirit" refers to the experience of common spontaneous song—a sung "word of praise." Some participants sing in tongues, others in their own language, and the Spirit weaves melodies with harmony, counterpoint, and dissonance which professional musicians envy. Occasionally an individual will sing an inspired song. Spontaneous singing not only opens a prayer meeting to praise, but it also develops joy in participants.

Leaders and participants should work hard at making their prayer meetings alive and responsive to the Holy Spirit's leadings. We should undergird our work with faith which enables the Lord to build a lively prayer meeting for us. When we notice something wrong or lacking, our first thought should be to turn to the Lord Jesus in prayer. Our second thought should be to do what we can to build along with him.

4

Helping Others Receive New Life

In the early church, Christians knew by experience that something had happened when they received the Holy Spirit. They could point to specific consequences of being baptized in the Holy Spirit. Christians were expected to be able to tell if they had experienced a release of the Holy Spirit or not. "Did you receive the Holy Spirit when you believed?" Paul once asked a group of Ephesian disciples. By observing their behavior, he suspected that they had not yet been baptized in the Holy Spirit. He expected them to be able to answer with a simple "yes" or "no," based upon events they could specify or changes they could notice.

> "No, we have never even heard that there is a Holy Spirit." And he said, "Into what then were you baptized?" They said, "into John's baptism." And Paul said, "John baptized with the baptism of repentance, telling the people to believe in one who was to come after him, that is, Jesus." On hearing this, they were baptized in the name of the Lord Jesus. And when Paul had laid his hands upon them, the Holy Spirit came on them; and they spoke with tongues and prophesied. (Acts 19:2-6)

Were we to ask Christians today if they had received the

Holy Spirit, many would be able to answer "yes" and point to God's action in their lives as proof. But many others would be puzzled by the question itself. They *know* that they received the Holy Spirit, but they cannot point to any evidence to convince the questioner or themselves. For example, Roman Catholics believe that Baptism and its complementary sacraments of initiation—Confirmation and the Eucharist—introduce a person into the divine life by conferring the Holy Spirit. Yet few Catholics would testify to a lasting personal experience of the Lord as a result of these sacraments. For several centuries, Catholic teaching has emphasized the power of the sacramental sign to affect an inner change. This teaching has led to a consequent de-emphasis on the importance of the right attitude of heart in the recipient. Too often, young people who had been baptized as infants are not called later to repentance and faith in the Lord as a way of bringing into their daily lives the divine power they had received sacramentally. For many, Baptism has been reduced to a ritual, with scarcely any practical consequences. The sacrament has its effect—the Holy Spirit comes to dwell in the heart of the recipient. But the recipient, sometimes through no fault of his own, allows the Spirit to lie latent within, failing to recognize his leadings and to cooperate with his power.

In our day, the Lord is acting decisively to renew Christian initiation. The church is rediscovering the importance of providing a comprehensive process of introducing people into the Christian life. Essential as they are, the sacraments only meet a person at a specific point in his life with Christ. He has spiritual needs before and after which the sacraments alone cannot satisfy. The church of the early centuries accumulated extensive practical wisdom about these needs. It learned that people who were becoming Christians needed to hear the good news and to have it explained, to enter supportive and orderly relationships with their brothers and sisters, to be set free from the influence of evil spirits, to receive instruction and experience in living the Christian life, and to receive and learn to exercise the charismatic gifts. The church came to regard Christian initiation as a process called the catechumenate. It included the sacraments along with many other elements of instruction, ministry, and spiritual nourishment. In the last decade, the Roman Catholic Church has been working towards the development of a new catechumenate to help contemporary Christians experience the fullness of the Christian life.

The charismatic renewal is contributing to the renewal of Christian initiation and to the renewal of the catechumenate. Being baptized in the Holy Spirit has helped many Christians tap the power God gave them sacramentally, but which they had not known how to use in their daily lives. Prayer groups have accumulated a considerable amount of practical experience in helping people receive and sustain a new life in the Spirit. In fact, developing a successful way to care for people who wanted to be baptized in the Spirit was a key factor allowing prayer groups to become stable enough to make a contribution to the spiritual renewal of the church.

A Way of Helping Others

At the beginning of the charismatic renewal, the Lord gave a release of the Holy Spirit to many baptized Christians who simply turned to him and asked for it. However, people soon began to gather in prayer meetings, and it became clear to the fledgling groups that Jesus wanted more care given to helping people receive new life in the Spirit.

In one early group I was associated with, many serious inquirers and curious observers attended the prayer meetings, some timidly hovering at doorways and lining the halls. At the end, those leading the meeting would invite anyone who wanted to be baptized in the Spirit to come to the center to be prayed with. One evening, so many of the onlookers came forward for prayer that the little prayer group reconsidered its policy. At a special meeting, those with responsibility for the meeting decided to stop praying with people at the end of the meeting and to start a special session afterwards. From that time on, anyone who was interested was invited to attend a short explanation after the prayer meeting. After hearing the talk, anyone who wished received prayer for a release of the Spirit.

The leaders made this important decision because they were concerned for the people who were expressing a desire to experience a new life in the Spirit. The Lord was free to release his Spirit in everyone without any involvement of the prayer group. Yet he seemed to want the group to take some responsibility for this work. In those early days, we were beginning to glimpse a truth which has since become much plainer to participants in the charismatic renewal: when we are bringing people to him to receive a new life in the Spirit, the Lord wants us to love them with his love, and care for them with his care. An unstructured, casual approach to praying with people may appear to be more spiritual, but it can be irresponsible and even unspiritual. The haphazard approach prayer groups took in the beginning allowed people to go away confused, and others to feel unworthy or rejected. We began to discover that taking a little time to explain helped people approach the Lord confidently and expectantly. Far from being unspiritual, an orderly pattern of initiation facilitated the work of the Holy Spirit.

Within two years, various groups had discovered that even a single explanation session did not provide sufficient care for those seeking to be baptized in the Spirit. Some groups started an additional session, giving more instruction and opportunity for questions, sharing, and discussion. At some point they began to suggest that new people visit mature members of the prayer group so that they might have some personal contact before being prayed with. Groups also began to offer short courses for people after they had been prayed with. "Growth Seminars" provided teaching and discussion on topics such as personal prayer, spiritual gifts, working through problems, and principles of spiritual growth.

This evolution of an intiations pattern reflected a deepening understanding of what the Lord seemed to be doing in the charismatic renewal. In the beginning, the casual approach to praying with people reflected the movement's emphasis on the new power of being baptized in the Holy Spirit. They tended to see the experience as "The Answer" and they eagerly and quickly brought others to receive a similar release of the Spirit. As the groups developed they began to understand that the Lord was not merely dispensing spiritual experience; he was offering a full renewal of the Christian life. Groups began to place being baptized in the Holy Spirit in a new perspective, seeing it less as a spiritual event and more as an important element in the process of living a full Christian life. Caring for new people came to mean more than praying with them. Groups were concerned to give adequate instruction, personal counseling, and teaching on spiritual growth.

In 1969, The Word of God, an ecumenical charismatic community in Ann Arbor, Michigan, pulled together various elements into an introductory unit called The Life in the Spirit Seminars. This short course included teaching, discussion, personal contact, and prayer. The community designed it as an instrument to provide the best available instruction and care for people who desired to be baptized in the Holy Spirit. In the past six years this particular way of helping people has come to be widely used in the charismatic renewal. Seventy-five thousand copies of the *Life in the Spirit Seminars Team Manual* are in print. More than a quarter million copies of the participants' handbook, *Finding New Life*, are in circulation. More than 10,000 of these booklets are sold each month. The Life in the Spirit Seminars have made a major contribution to the growth of the charismatic renewal.

The Goal of the Life in the Spirit Seminars

By the time The Word of God developed the Life in the Spirit Seminars, the community had already placed being baptized in the Holy Spirit in a wider context. The community had come to view the purpose of the course as a way to help people find new life, not simply as a way to provide a spiritual experience. Offering an opportunity to pray for a release of the Holy Spirit was regarded as one among several important elements leading toward this goal.

The goal of the Life in the Spirit Seminars is to help people establish, re-establish, or strengthen the foundation of their lives on the Lord Jesus Christ. All men have varying specific personal needs, but all have in common the fundamental need to have their lives centered in Jesus. "For no other foundation can anyone lay than that which is laid, which is Jesus Christ" (1 Cor. 3:11). All of the elements of the seminar work together to help a person establish this foundation and to live a life in the Holy Spirit.

To help people achieve this goal, the Life in the Spirit Seminars provide four significant opportunities. First, the seminars are designed to enable people to enter into a personal relationship with God. Many people among us are not aware that they can come to know Jesus, experience his love, and allow him to govern their lives. This group includes many good Christian men and women who love God and obey him, but who for some reason have never met the Lord as a person. The Life in the Spirit Seminars create an environment in which people can discover the Lord and encounter him in a new personal relationship. It brings people into contact with Christians who know Jesus and who speak about him in a way which invites others to seek him. Those who do not know God at all have an opportunity to find him; those who once knew him but have drifted away can renew contact with him; those who know him already can deepen their relationship.

Second, the Life in the Spirit Seminars assist people in yielding to the action of the Holy Spirit in their lives. Far too many of us have tried to live our Christian lives on our own power. We try to force ourselves to obey the law by sheer willpower. We have a Rolls Royce, but we laboriously push it along from behind. We get somewhere, but not very far. Paul exposes the folly of this law approach in the seventh and eighth chapters of Romans. He shows us the great spiritual power we have if we will learn to use it. Faith, like a key in the ignition, opens us to the powerful action of the Holy Spirit. The Life in the Spirit Seminars show people through teaching and personal contact what it means to yield to the Spirit. They also help build the faith necessary to free the Spirit to work.

Third, the seminars help people move on toward Christian maturity by teaching them how to use essential means of spiritual growth. A garden which is well watered but otherwise untended will soon be choked with weeds, bear little fruit, and go to seed. Similarly, a Christian's life will also bear little fruit if he fails to make faithful use of the means for growth which the Lord has given us. This is true even for people who know Jesus and are baptized in the Holy Spirit. Personal prayer, corporate worship and sacraments, fellowship with brothers and sisters, service to each other and to society, study of Scripture and spiritual reading—all are essentials for our maturing in Christ. The Life in the Spirit Seminars support people in deciding to use these means for growth through straightforward teaching, exhortation, and especially through the encouraging example of men and women who are already using these means to grow in the Spirit.

Finally, the Life in the Spirit Seminars bring people into relationships with men and women who are living in Christian brotherhood. Our Christian lives require the support of brothers and sisters who have made some commitment to love and serve us. Our ordinary social environments do not support efforts to live a life in the Spirit. The values and patterns of behavior in our normal situations can draw us away from the Lord and prevent us from growing, obeying him, and making the changes in our life which he wants. The environment can seduce us into familiar wrongdoing or depress us with habitual discouragement. Nevertheless, the Lord wants us to live and work within our society. Thus regular sharing with others who are committed to Jesus and to us makes us resilient, enables us to move ahead with the Lord, and provides us with a source of practical wisdom. These relationships start forming during the Life in the Spirit Seminars. Friendships built at this time can be important initial connections which bring people into contact with the brotherhood which the Lord is building in his church.

The Talks, Discussions, and Personal Contact

The Life in the Spirit Seminars resemble the early Christian catechumenates. Like the catechumenate, the course is a way of bringing people into a new life in the Holy Spirit which leads to Christian maturity. Both are processes of Christian initiation which combine similar essential elements: proclamation of the good news, basic instruction, appropriation of new life in the Spirit, and incorporation into a body of Christians. The Life in the Spirit Seminars meet once each week for seven weeks for talks, discussions, prayer, and sharing. The seminar is designed to accomplish the four parts of initiation: proclamation, instruction, appropriation, and incorporation.

The first four talks are a systematic declaration of the good news. God is presented in the first talk as a loving Father who calls us to come to know, love, and serve him. The second talk shows that our salvation through the death and resurrection of Jesus transforms every dimension of our lives. The subjects of the third and fourth talks are how to turn to the Lord in repentance and faith and how to yield to the Holy Spirit. While all four presentations proclaim the gospel, the last two focus on how to appropriate the new life which the Lord offers.

Each talk is followed by discussions in small groups. All participants share reflections on some main points of the talk, ask questions of the discussion leader, share their experiences, and make observations. These discussions help people see the truth more clearly and prepare them to decide to make it their own. Between the fourth and fifth weeks of the seminar, each participant spends some time talking personally with the discussion leader. This personal contact helps determine if the individual is ready to be prayed with for being baptized in the Holy Spirit. The personal visit is another way in which the Life in the Spirit Seminars help a group actively assist people in entering into a new relationship with God.

Along with explanations, discussions, and the personal visit, a key event in helping people receive God's gift of new life is the fifth seminar itself. During the fifth session, participants are invited to give their lives anew to the Lord Jesus and to pray for a release of the Holy Spirit in their lives. The fifth seminar begins with a short talk. Participants then renew their baptismal vows, and recite a prayer of dedication to the Lord which concludes by asking him to baptize them in the Holy Spirit and to give them the gift of tongues. A period of spontaneous prayer follows, during which seminar leaders may lay hands upon those who are seeking a release of the Holy Spirit.

Talks six and seven of these seminars are best described as basic instruction for Christian living. Here participants learn practical wisdom about using the essential means for growth which the Lord has given us. They also hear about dealing with common problems encountered in daily Christian life, problems such as doubt and temptation. This instruction is by no means comprehensive and is intended only as a foundation for growth.

For our purpose of understanding the Life in the Spirit Seminars, "incorporation" means developing a relationship with a prayer group, not inclusion in the body of Christ or membership in the church as it did in the catechumenate. The seventh talk performs a small part of the function of incorporating people by explaining how they can become a part of the prayer group. However, people become part of a prayer group not so much through teaching as through personal contact. Interaction with prayer group members which fosters friendships is a very important part of the Life in the Spirit Seminars. Some prayer groups involve many of their members in simply building informal friendly relations with the seminar participants.

Hearing the good news, receiving basic teaching, learning how to appropriate God's gifts, and coming into committed relationships—these are essential elements of initiation which are built into the Life in the Spirit Seminars. There are other essentials such as water baptism and eucharistic worship which the Life in the Spirit Seminars do not provide. Water baptism and the Eucharist are rites of initiation which are provided by churches and congregations.

Life in the Spirit Seminars are bringing spiritual renewal to many adult Christians. Because the prayer groups which offer these seminars are fully committed to the church, the Life in the Spirit Seminars can be viewed as an important part of the church's efforts to renew initiation.

Adapting the Life in the Spirit Seminars

The Life in the Spirit Seminars have proven to be an instrument which any prayer group can use. Prayer groups of all sizes and kinds have tailored the course to fit their purposes. A prayer group can successfully imitate the practice of groups roughly similar to itself as long as the leaders take the group's particular needs and resources into account.

Prayer groups around the world use the Life in the Spirit Seminars in very different ways. Some small prayer groups—those with less than 40 members—begin by presenting the Seminars for the whole group as a part of its weekly prayer meeting. These smaller groups then offer additional seminars only when there are about 10 or so people who want to take them. Some very small groups send people to a larger prayer group nearby instead of offering the Life in the Spirit Seminars themselves. Some larger prayer groups have two and sometimes three Life in the Spirit Seminars being conducted at the same time. They serve more people and may have to begin a new seminar shortly after one series has started. Other groups present the Life in the Spirit Seminars on a retreat weekend. The weekend format is particularly desirable in rural areas where people cannot travel great distances every week, or in places where poverty prevents extensive travel. In such cases, those offering the weekend should take special care to make sure that seminar participants are incorporated into an active Christian body.

Prayer groups which decide to use the Life in the Spirit Seminars should carefully integrate them into their life. Choosing to offer the seminars is an important step and should be the

responsibility of the recognized leaders team. The leaders team should plan the use of the seminars carefully, prepare the prayer group, establish a basic pattern for putting on the series, choose and train teachers and discussion leaders, develop ways of connecting people who complete the seminars with the group, and maintain close contact with the program once it is initiated.

This planning for the Life in the Spirit Seminars involves both settling practical details and coming to a clearer understanding of the purpose of the prayer group. Since Life in the Spirit Seminars are intended to help people come into the life of a prayer group, it is helpful for people in the prayer group to have some understanding of what the Lord is doing with them and what he is calling them to. For example, if one purpose of the seminars is to join new people to the prayer group, then the group should have a clear idea of what commitment to the group means. This should help people decide more easily if they want to become members. Settling these questions about the direction of the group assists prayer groups in a wise use of the Life in the Spirit Seminars.

Many practical questions must be answered before a prayer group can begin using Life in the Spirit Seminars. When should the seminar meet? Some prayer groups have the Life in the Spirit Seminars before the weekly prayer meeting; some have it afterwards; others have it on another night. How frequently should the prayer group offer a seminar? Frequency of the seminars depends upon both the availability of capable people to present the course, and a sufficient number of people who want to take it. The more important of these considerations is the first. If a capable team is not available, new people should be asked to wait. How many people should be in a seminar? Some groups limit the number to about 10. On the other extreme, some groups have handled 100. The size of the seminar depends on the size of the team. Rarely should one team member have to care for more than four or five people.

These are only a few of the questions which should be settled by the leaders team. Other questions include how to conduct the fifth week of the seminar, who should be teaching and leading discussions, where to hold the sessions, and how to be sure new people come in contact with the prayer group members.

In summary, a good approach to planning the Life in the Spirit Seminars must be comprehensive. It involves settling the broad questions about the nature of the prayer group; defining the limits of its resources; studying all relevant material such as the *Team Manual for the Life in the Spirit Seminars* and other useful books and tapes; making all practical arrangements before the program begins; and consulting with sound and experienced neighboring prayer groups.

As a part of the planning process, the leaders team should work out a tentative pattern for using the seminars in the prayer group. This pattern is the summary of the answers to all of the necessary questions. This basic plan should be realistic and within the limits set by the size of the group and the availability of capable people. Also, the leaders team should expect to make changes in this pattern as the group acquires experience in presenting the seminars. For example, the Grand Haven group originally offered a new Life in the Spirit Seminar every three weeks. Then the demand slackened and the leaders team decided that the seminar teams were overworked. Eventually, after several years of adjustment, the Grand Haven leaders settled on this plan for the seminars. We decided to offer the Life in the Spirit Seminars before the prayer meetings; not to begin a new seminar until after the previous one ended; to have a member of the leaders team teach each seminar; to limit the number in the course to three or four per discussion leader; and to have a team meeting each week.

The leaders team should prepare the prayer group for the use of Life in the Spirit Seminars by teaching about Christian initiation and the importance of an orderly way of helping people appropriate new life. Leaders teams should be sure that the whole prayer group sees being baptized in the Spirit not as an end but as a source of life which leads to maturity in Christ. Talks, general discussions, and small group discussions on these subjects will benefit the whole prayer group. When a prayer group decides to use the Life in the Spirit Seminars, all members should accept them as the normal way of helping people receive a release of the Holy Spirit. Ordinarily, people in the prayer group would not pray with others who desire to be baptized in the Spirit, but would invite them to attend the seminars. This policy assures that the prayer group is taking responsibility for the people prayed for. Since being baptized in the Spirit is an opening to new life, rather than simply a spiritual experience, it is something that should ordinarily occur within the prayer group, not with one or two other people.

Acquiring Skills for Helping Others

After prayer groups have presented Life in the Spirit Seminars for a while, they accumulate substantial practical wisdom about helping others experience and grow in a new life in the Spirit. Groups and leaders should consciously try to increase their understanding of the initiation process through evaluation, study, training, and sharing of experiences. These steps will develop pastoral skills and make us more responsible servants.

A method of evaluation should be built into the planning of the seminars. Each week the team presenting a particular Life in the Spirit Seminar should briefly evaluate the effectiveness of the previous week's presentation and discussions. The team leader should make note of both positive appraisals and constructive criticism so that he can improve his own skills and recommend changes to the leaders team. Team members should be able to compliment and correct each other during the evaluation sessions. For example, if the speaker covered the material thoroughly but gave some weak illustrations, the team should praise him for the one and show him how to improve the other. The leaders team should conduct regular evaluations of the whole initiations process. Maintaining records and keeping in contact with people who complete the seminar help in determining the effectiveness of the seminars. The leaders team should want to know what happened to people who attended the Life in the Spirit Seminars and the type of relationship they have with the prayer group. People who complete the course may be asked to help evaluate the process. Those who drift away from the prayer group may also be asked for their evaluation of the seminars. The seminar teams may be asked for their reflections on the strengths and weaknesses of the process.

Such information will show the leaders team how to improve the Life in the Spirit Seminars. Performing the evaluation will also broaden the pastoral skill of everyone involved.

Reflecting on the effectiveness of our service as individuals and as groups is an important instrument of growth. Individuals can become better servants by regular and careful examination of their work. For example, a discussion leader can learn more from his experience in leading discussions if he reviews his work regularly.

A few years ago I faced the question of how to show others how to lead seminar discussions effectively. I felt that I did a reasonably good job in leading discussions myself and wanted to share what I knew. But my initial impulse, before reflecting about my job, was to advise people to simply jump in and start leading discussions. However, I spent some time thinking about the many experiences—both good and bad—I had had in discussions. I soon discovered that I had at my disposal a rich resource of practical wisdom about discussions which had remained untapped until I began to reflect on specific experiences.

Reflecting on the experience of individuals who attend the Life in the Spirit Seminars can teach us a great deal about helping others. For example, if we find that young people seem to receive more from the seminars than older people do, a careful consideration of how we work with the young may help us improve our service to those who are older. Team members can both develop their skills and grow in understanding by serious consideration of their practice and the experience of people they serve.

Study about Christian initiation in general and about the Life in the Spirit Seminars in particular is a valuable way to broaden the pastoral wisdom of the prayer group. All concerned with helping others should have read and discussed the *Team Manual*. Those who have overall responsibility for initiations should do serious reading in theological, scriptural, and pastoral works. Discussion with leaders of neighboring groups and participation in workshops on initiations can be very useful forms of study.

Pastoral skill in helping others can be communicated to new leaders through experience and training. People who are to become seminar discussion leaders can begin by serving as assistants to experienced discussion leaders. By observation and limited involvement, they will learn enough to begin leading discussions themselves. Prayer groups can train new team members through instruction based on a study of the *Team Manual* and use of tapes such as those recommended at the end of this book. However, there is no better training than actually doing the work and evaluating it faithfully.

A Brotherly Approach

Experience shows that Life in the Spirit Seminars can become lifeless and mechanical if we do not approach new people with love, attention, and faith. The name "seminar" itself suggests an academic activity; when we approach the Life in the Spirit Seminars purely as a teaching service, they can become as sterile as a dull classroom situation. Teaching is an important part of the course, but only a part and not the most important at that. On the other hand, groups may take an overspiritual approach to the Life in the Spirit Seminars, regarding themselves as dispensers of God's gifts. This is a false notion which must be rejected. The healthiest view is this: the Life in the Spirit Seminars are an opportunity for brothers and sisters to enter into a new and deeper relationship with the

Lord. The prayer group members serving on the seminar function together to create an environment which draws people into contact with Jesus. Those working on the Life in the Spirit Seminars should not regard themselves either as teachers or as the specially gifted, but as servants befriending people in the name of the Lord. The work of the seminar team is essential if the Life in the Spirit Seminars are to function as a brotherhood, including people in its relationship with Jesus and inviting them to find a new life in the Spirit. Practically speaking, this means that the team must work together in unity, serving each other, expressing affection openly, and be in good personal relationships.

Sometimes prayer groups have allowed the Life in the Spirit Seminars to become mechanical by their failure to pay personal attention to the people they are serving. These groups have approached the initiations process as though it were a spiritual assembly line, with specific things being done to people at different points. While the Life in the Spirit Seminars involve a series of definite events, we should not become so absorbed in the prescribed pattern that we lose sight of the people. We need to have the Lord's perspective. He does not approach us as objects that he does something to. He approaches us as brothers and sisters whom he loves. He does not blur us into a crowd; he sees us and appreciates us as unique persons. We should learn to see the people coming to the Life in the Spirit Seminars in the same way, being sensitive to them and appreciating them as individuals. No two people we serve are identical. No two people are in exactly the same relationship to the Lord. The good news cannot be squeezed into a formula with universal application. Those serving on the seminar team must learn to approach every person as unique and to tailor the expression of the gospel to meet him where he is.

Sometimes groups allow the Life in the Spirit Seminars to become mechanical by letting them solidify into a routine. We

can easily fall into the trap of putting more faith in the seminar than in the Lord. If we do this, we can expect the process of initiation to come to a stop. The Life in the Spirit Seminars are simply a framework designed to allow the Holy Spirit freedom to work. The team should not be startled when the Holy Spirit presents them with surprises. He is not to be limited by our narrow expectations or our schedules. Participants should be encouraged at the very first session to seek the Lord and to expect the Lord to work differently and personally in every seminar. Further, the team should count on the Lord to provide them with the practical wisdom they need to perform their service responsibly. Because he cares for both participants and team members, the Lord will equip the team with all the gifts they must have in order to work well along with him. "If any of you lacks wisdom, let him ask God, who gives to all men generously and without reproaching, and it will be given him" (James 1:5).

5

Providing Teaching

One of the surprises of the Holy Spirit for people who become involved in the charismatic renewal is a craving for substantial teaching on how to live the Christian life. Being baptized in the Holy Spirit transforms people who have had no interest in religious education into insatiable students. They discover that they do not yet know how to live the new life in the Spirit which the Lord has opened to them.

Spiritual experience without basic teaching is somewhat like running in place—one wastes energy but gets nowhere. Unfortunately, many who begin to experience a spiritual renewal are in exactly this condition: their spiritual experience goes to waste because they do not learn how to grow spiritually. Prayer groups that lead people into being baptized in the Holy Spirit have a responsibility to provide regular teaching to help new people learn to live their new life in the Spirit. Presenting basic instruction on Christian living is difficult; not all prayer groups are equipped to do it well on their own. But since sound teaching is a matter of spiritual life or death, providing it is a challenge we must meet.

Christian Maturity

Basic teaching is the single most important part of the process of helping people grow to maturity in Christ. The Holy Spirit wants to form people in Christian living just as parents want to form their children in good habits of practical living. Parents discover by experience that direct instruction of the child works more effectively than indirect suggestions or mere good example. For example, I could attempt to form my children in honesty and respect for the truth by simply always being honest and never lying; I could try to be a good example. But without my teaching on the subject, my children could absorb the influences of their peers and eventually decide that their honest father was only hopelessly naive. Just as authoritative communication of the truth about living is essential to form children, authoritative teaching is equally essential to form Christians.

The way parents teach their children is determined by the kind of person they want their child to become. In the same way, the content of Christian teaching is shaped by the image of the mature Christian. We want our sons and daughters to be upright, honest, self-controlled, faithful, and loving. When we teach them, we have in mind the excellent men and woman they will become. Similarly, when prayer groups teach, they have in mind the final product—the mature sons and daughters Jesus wants to present to his father.

Thus, prayer groups can understand what basic teaching should include by reflecting on the characteristics of a mature Christian. What are these characteristics? The mature Christian consistently loves God above everything and obeys him habitually. He loves his fellow Christians with a consistently high degree of commitment to serve them unselfishly, and he loves his neighbor as well. He is a servant who always places the interests of others before his own. He knows how to find the truth in Scripture and the church's tradition and how to receive the guidance of the Holy Spirit. He has an active faith which enables him to tap God's power and receive spiritual gifts. He makes consistent use of the means of growth—daily prayer, study, sacramental worship, and fellowship. The mature Christian manifests the marks of Christian character:

love, joy, peace, patience, kindness, gentleness, generosity, faithfulness, and self-control, to name only a few. He understands the causes of his problems and knows how to overcome them. He maintains right relationships with everyone in his social environment and knows how to repair broken relationships when they occur. He has a love for the church, has an appreciation for the Lord's plan, and is assuming his place of service in it.

Basic teaching is the road to Christian maturity. Basic Christian instruction must cover such topics as making God the priority, Christian love, faith, understanding Scripture, Christian character, right relationships, and handling problems. Normally this type of foundational teaching is concerned with practical wisdom, with the "how to's" more than the "whys." However, people will often more readily accept the advice if they also understand the scriptural and theological truths behind it.

Prayer groups which are not yet able to provide such a comprehensive teaching should not become discouraged. Later we shall describe resources which any prayer group can use to provide a course of basic teaching.

Sustenance and Growth

Teaching is also essential for the welfare of the prayer group as a whole. Basic instruction is a way to both sustain the prayer group's life and to move it ahead in response to the Lord's leadings.

Regular teaching is important for the "upkeep" of the prayer group. The prayer group's spiritual health depends upon paying faithful attention to every essential part of its corporate activity. For example, participants should hear regular instruction on how to participate in the prayer meeting, how to use their spiritual gifts wisely, how to greet newcomers, and other vital subjects. Without this kind of maintenance of the group's life, people soon forget what the Lord has taught, and important elements of the group's life will die.

Teaching also maintains the quality of the prayer group's life by helping newcomers participate fully. As they mature, prayer groups develop to a point where it is difficult for newcomers to fully enter the group's life unless they receive adequate explanation. For example, in most prayer groups, everyone is committed to a daily personal prayer time. Yet newcomers cannot be expected to undertake such a practice unless someone teaches them about the importance of prayer, how to pray, and the other information that others in the group already know. This holds true in many other areas of the group's life. If prayer groups fail to teach newcomers, they will soon become weaker and will loose their sense of direction.

In many prayer groups, the Lord seems to be using teaching to renew the experience of unity among Christians, something he prayed would characterize the body of his disciples. Unity in prayer groups is a oneness created out of commitment to the Lord and to brothers and sisters. Teaching helps to maintain unity by communicating to all an understanding of the Lord's call to the group. Regular instruction on the simple truths of practical Christian living also forms a common mind in the group which brings a daily flow of strength to all the members. Thus, calling forth oneness is both a reason and a goal for providing teaching.

Teaching is essential for giving direction to a prayer group. Leaders teams must teach with authority in order to keep the group on the right path, to correct it, to make changes in direction, to alter its pattern of life, and to move it ahead in response to the Spirit's leading. Teaching gives people the understanding and motivation which enable them to accept change and correction. Without instruction, efforts to move the group along will produce fear, suspicion, and division.

For example, teaching can help a prayer group accomplish

one of its most difficult jobs: changing the form and membership of leaders teams. With adequate explanation to the whole group, the job of making adjustments in leaders teams can be made considerably easier. Twice the Grand Haven prayer group reached a decision to make changes in the structure of the team and in its membership. The first time, a number of people in the prayer group were confused and hurt unnecessarily because the leaders failed to give adequate teaching about the changes. Five years later, when it again seemed necessary to make significant changes in the organization and membership of the team, we did not make the same mistake. The leaders explained everything to the members of the prayer group, gave teaching on choosing leaders, and consulted with the group through discussions. The changes occurred peacefully and a stronger group resulted. The Grand Haven experience illustrated an important point: without teaching, adequate direction of prayer groups is impossible.

Recognizing Teachers

As important as it is, providing teaching is often the weakest part of a prayer group's life. The ability to teach is a spiritual gift. Not all prayer groups have people who have this gift and can give instruction effectively. Developing teaching is also a very difficult task which many groups do not have the internal resources to undertake. However, such obstacles must not prevent prayer groups from providing teaching. Leaders teams should evaluate the group's teaching. If there is no teaching, they should formulate a plan to make instruction a regular part of the prayer group's activity. If the teaching is inadequate, the leaders team should take steps to improve it.

Prayer groups should learn to identify people with a teaching gift. Criteria which indicate that a person has a gift to give instruction include natural ability, pastoral and spiritual gifts, effects of his teaching, educational background, and personal

Christian maturity. Normally the Lord will give teaching gifts to individuals who have a natural clarity of thought and speech which enables them to instruct others effectively. The person the Lord chooses for this service is likely to be someone who speaks and thinks clearly, although this person will not necessarily be a teacher by profession. Not everyone, in fact, who has received specialized academic training will be called to teach in prayer groups. Some professional teachers receive the gift, but others do not. The priest or minister is a special case in this regard. His theological training is a valuable asset which he should use to advise the prayer group, but his education alone does not equip him for teaching. Some priests and ministers have gifts for teaching, but others have different gifts. Prayer groups should not assume that every clergyman who attends regularly should automatically become a teacher. Such an assumption is unfair to him and the prayer group. The presence of the gift—not a person's state in life—is the criterion for identifying a teacher.

A teacher should have some of the same gifts that members of the leaders team manifest. A good teacher has a sense of what the prayer group needs to hear now and some sense of what the Lord wants to communicate to it. He knows how to speak to the prayer group in ways which bring good responses. For example, he should be able to give a strong correction which leads the group to reform rather than to be discouraged. Often people with teaching gifts are also equipped with the spiritual gifts of the word of wisdom and the word of knowledge. The word of wisdom is the understanding which the Lord brings to the teacher's mind as he speaks. The word of knowledge is the insight the teacher receives into Christian truths which strengthens his instruction.

A teacher can also be identified by the results of his teaching. A good teacher's instruction will produce faith, understanding, and action in those who hear him. By its acceptance, the prayer group as a whole should be able to say that the teacher is a person whose teaching has a positive impact on their lives. Individual members of prayer groups should tell the leaders team when they notice that they are benefitting from someone's teaching.

In his own personal life, the teacher should be advancing to full Christian maturity. He should bear the same marks of Christian character expected of all Christian leaders, especially since his words will begin to direct the prayer groups as a rudder guides a ship. The same criteria discussed in chapter two for determining who should serve on leaders teams should be applied to potential teachers (see pp. 38-43).

Prayer groups should be especially wary of visiting teachers who may have a strong spiritual gift, but whose personal lives are unknown to the group. Only teachers with a sound reputation should be allowed to give teaching. While some traveling teachers have a call from God, others travel to escape their reputations. Leaders teams should exercise discernment and have the courage to ask unknown visitors not to teach at their prayer meeting.

Prayer groups that find people with teaching gifts among their members should allow them opportunities for development. The leaders team should regularly invite gifted people to give short teachings during the weekly prayer meeting. As the individual teachers grow, they should begin to help the leaders team to oversee the content of teaching and to develop courses for instruction.

Regular meetings of all those who give teaching will help foster the gift in the prayer group. Teachers should evaluate talks together and learn how to speak more effectively. Such a meeting is an opportunity for prayer, specifically seeking the Lord's vision for the prayer group. Teachers should also study and discuss tapes and books as a way of improving their teaching.

Developing Courses

In well-organized, mature prayer groups, the leaders team and teachers may develop courses of instruction as ways of providing basic instruction. A full-scale discussion of how to develop courses is beyond the scope of this chapter, but the following advice suggests a sound approach.

First, the content of courses should normally be determined by a team. Conducting study sessions on the subject, with a careful use of brainstorming and discussion, will help guarantee the quality of the teaching. After the topic is thoroughly discussed, one person or a smaller committee many be assigned to draw up a detailed outline which presents the material in an orderly way.

This team approach was used very effectively in developing the teaching for regional service conferences which were given for leaders throughout the U.S.A. in the early years of the charismatic renewal. A team discussed the proposed topic at length; one person or a small committee then organized the material into outlines and commentaries. The original team read the proposed outlines and offered suggestions for improvement. After the service conferences were presented a few times, the original group met to evaluate the teaching and offer further advice. The same procedure works in prayer groups. A team will prepare a course more thoroughly than one person can, and the teaching will thus be as complete and correct as possible. The practice of assigning a smaller group or even one person to organize the material into a course helps to unify and integrate the content.

A second principle for developing teaching should be to seek wisdom about how to discover and explain basic Christian truths. The chief source of this wisdom is the Holy Spirit. He teaches us through the Scriptures, through the teaching of the church, through the experience of others, and through our own lives. However, getting at the truth is not automatic. Correct interpretation of a Scripture and proper understanding of tradition and experience require not only spiritual gifts, but also study skills and disciplined minds. Leaders teams and teachers who neglect study and the training of their minds would be irresponsible.

Third, teams should make intelligent use of available resources. Many prayer groups have already developed courses which provide excellent models of teaching. Many books, both old and new, offer wisdom on living the Christian life. Other media—particularly cassettes—present additional resource material. Our use of models, books, tapes, and other resources should be both open and critical. We should be eager to learn from others, but critical enough to recognize and reject what is unhelpful or false.

Fourth, those preparing courses should give careful consideration to relating basic Christian truths to the particular situation of the local prayer group. The application of basic Christian teaching itself depends upon individual circumstances. Some useful questions leaders should ask when adapting a piece of basic teaching are: 1) Where is the prayer group's teaching in need of development? Does the prayer group lack teaching in this area? 2) What does the Lord want to accomplish in the group now? Is the timing right for introducing this teaching? 3) Can the members of the prayer group be expected to apply this teaching in their lives? Is there something in the local situation which would prevent them from following this instruction? 4) Will this teaching as we are presenting it have the correct impact on the prayer group? 5) What can we do to help prayer group members apply this teaching?

Finally, the team must continually evaluate and maintain the content of the courses. Once a set of teachings is presented a few times, the team should evaluate the series and take steps to improve it. As new courses are added to strengthen the maturing prayer group, the team must be sure that the courses are consistent and complementary. They must see to it that all important subjects are treated somewhere in the series of courses.

More extensive advice on preparing courses is available in the books and cassettes in the recommended list for this chapter (see pp. 125-126). Developing courses is not easy. It requires gifted people and constant pastoral care. Prayer groups who decide to move in this direction should be sure in advance that they have adequate resources—a good leaders team and gifted teachers.

Making Use of Available Teaching

The lack of gifted teachers does not excuse the prayer group from taking responsibility for providing teaching. Since teaching is a spiritual gift, the prayer group should pray and expect the Lord to meet its needs, perhaps by developing teachers in the group. At the same time, prayer groups should use all available resources to present teaching to the group.

Even if no gifted teachers are present, nothing should prevent the leaders team from giving direction to the entire prayer group. The chairman of the leaders team or the team member who speaks most clearly should regularly talk to the group about its purpose, life, and activities. He or she should trust the Lord to bring about the appropriate response in the prayer group.

Most prayer groups are small enough to make effective use of available teaching on cassette recordings. Some prayer groups listen to a taped talk or a portion of a talk before or after their prayer meeting. The leaders team must invest a significant amount of time in order to use tapes responsibly. Because cassettes are somewhat impersonal, the team must educate the prayer group to expect the Lord to work through the teaching. They may need to exhort the participants to work harder at paying attention than they would when listening to a live speaker. Some effort must be spent in obtaining the best available sound equipment to assure that everyone will be able to hear without difficulty.

Most important, the team must evaluate the teachings beforehand so that it can exercise pastoral judgment on their content. When the team discovers some weakness in a talk, it may decide not to present it to the group, or they may decide to caution the group about questionable parts, correcting mistakes. Some teaching on a particular cassette may not apply to the local situation. The leaders team should help the prayer group adapt the advice or indicate which advice to ignore. Because there is an ever-growing supply of teaching on cassettes, leaders teams must be diligent in discerning in the talks to be played for the prayer group.

Discussion is an integral part of instruction because it is an opportunity for people to fully appropriate teaching. Talks frequently have no impact because some people have not learned how to apply teaching. Discussion enables a person to seek explanation for a point he did not understand. It also creates a situation in which he can grasp points which otherwise would elude him. However, discussion is normally inappropriate after a teaching delivered during a prayer meeting; prayer meetings are for praising God. Instead, the leader should exhort the gathering to respond to the message in an appropriate way. But many prayer groups wisely provide discussion periods as a part of all courses and after presenting cassettes. Sharing about a taped talk with others is especially valuable because discussion helps overcome the impersonal quality of receiving teaching from a tape recorder.

Some prayer groups provide teaching through the discussion of Scripture or books. Discussing parts of the Bible prayerfully and with the aid of commentaries is an excellent source of teaching. Other times, groups may choose to study a book together and discuss parts of it each week before the prayer meeting. In one group, the Lord worked major changes in the marriages and family life of the group's members through the discussion of books and cassettes on these topics. The leaders team should be responsible for helping discussion groups by providing discussion leaders and by helping select appropriate books.

In areas where a great number of small prayer groups have appeared, regional service centers are forming to provide teaching resources for the benefit of all local groups. In New Jersey, Ignatius House Community (Rutherford) and the People of H.O.P.E. (Convent Station) once each month offer teachings which members of nearby prayer groups can attend. Days of renewal in Detroit and in many other areas provide a monthly opportunity for small prayer groups to obtain good teaching. In Los Angeles and New Orleans, area-wide service teams offer training for teachers in small prayer groups. Small prayer groups should look to each other for support in obtaining teaching resources and make use of regional services when they are available. Where cooperative teaching services are not available, leaders teams should give serious consideration to bringing together neighboring leaders to explore what might be possible.

The bibliography for this chapter at the end of the book suggests books and tapes which prayer groups may choose to use as resources for providing teaching. Outstanding among them is *The Foundations of Christian Living*. Under this title, The Word of God (Ann Arbor, Michigan) is publishing on cassette and in booklets various sets of talks developed as a part of its community life. *The Foundations of Christian Living* is basic teaching, offering practical advice important to any follower of Jesus Christ. "Basic Christian Maturity," known popularly as "Foundations I," is a cassette album with leaders guide designed to lay the groundwork for additional sets in the series.

Providing teaching is one of the more difficult challenges prayer groups face. Identifying teachers, developing courses, adapting existing materials, discerning the prayer group's needs, evaluation—all of the activities involved in the process require work and grace. But no reward is more satisfying than watching people grow to maturity in Christ in response to basic teaching. As Christians grow to maturity, renewal spreads throughout the church.

6

Making Love Your Aim

Christianity, by God's design, is a system of personal relationships among the brothers and sisters of the Lord. When Jesus prayed for our unity (John 17:21) and commanded us to love one another as he loved us (John 13:34), he was not speaking of something invisible or abstract. He was calling us to form a body which others could see. He intended that people would come to believe that the Father had sent him by observing the quality of our relationships with each other. Charismatic prayer groups are experiencing a renewal of this dimension of the church's life and promise to renew it throughout Christianity.

Building brotherly relationships is not easy, but the Lord has given us powerful resources to enable us to do it. Prayer groups should devote a maximum of effort to helping members learn to love one another, since love is the goal of Christian life. Prayer groups are in a position to make a major contribution to church renewal by faithfully employing every possible way of fostering personal relationships among their members.

Opportunities for Brotherhood

The characteristic meetings of the charismatic renewal can easily become ends in themselves. A prayer group can organize a prayer meeting, leaders team meetings, a monthly day of renewal, a Life in the Spirit Seminar, and numerous other meetings and end up with an intricate, but lifeless structure.

Meetings are important, but they lose value when they fail to serve a purpose higher than themselves. This purpose is love.

Prayer groups are environments which support people in loving the Lord and loving their brothers and sisters. All the meetings and activities of the group should be designed to enable people to grow in love. Prayer group members should never regard meetings as obligations, but as opportunities for developing personal relationships. Thus, leaders teams should take a hard look at the pattern of the group's meetings and activities to make sure that love, not meeting, is the prayer group's aim.

Prayer groups should provide members with ample opportunities to develop brotherly relationships with each other. The open prayer meeting in particular should provide occasion before and after for some informal sharing. If participants are finding it difficult to interact at the prayer meeting, the leaders team should consider changing its schedule or structure. A two-hour meeting could be cut to one-and-a-half hours to allow time at the end for sharing. A meeting beginning at 9 p.m. could be moved to 8:15 p.m., so that people would not have to rush home when it ends. Simple adjustments such as these can make major contributions to building brotherhood in the prayer group.

The prayer group should encourage members to come together informally as often as possible during the week. Families and single people should invite others to join them for meals. Parties, picnics, and all forms of recreation provide excellent opportunities for developing personal relationships. Helping each other with work, caring for each other's children, and undertaking service projects such as visiting the sick can also be significant ways of building brotherhood among prayer group members. Leaders teams should exhort every member to look for ways of having as much informal contact as possible with others in the prayer group.

Members of prayer groups will discover that they must gather frequently and in a variety of ways in order to foster brotherhood adequately. Experience has taught many groups that a weekly prayer meeting in itself does not allow enough time for creating committed relationships among participants. Groups have also learned that prayer meetings which are typically oriented to serving newcomers cannot meet the desires of more mature members for deeper commitment to one another.

To meet these needs for a deeper brotherly commitment, many prayer groups have started a second weekly meeting restricted to regular members of the group. This additional meeting not only enables members to grow in commitment to one another, but also allows the prayer group to meet its members' needs for teaching, Scripture study, fellowship, and other requirements. Newcomers are not invited to this second meeting so that participants may be free to focus entirely on the Lord and upon caring for each other. Prayer groups often call this second gathering the "core" meeting or the "community" meeting.

Frequently the community meeting is simply a prayer meeting. Members of the group gather before the Lord; he speaks to them, encourages them, corrects, heals, and calls them on with him. Often, groups find that the second meeting creates a strong sense of unity among members and strengthens them in their individual Christian lives. Being together a second time each week establishes broader and deeper relationships among participants.

Many prayer groups design their community meetings to accomplish several other purposes in addition to the prayer meeting. They may schedule time for regular teachings, sharing sessions, service meetings, and other activities. They often have refreshments and time for informal conversation at the conclusion of the meetings. Sometimes the group will share a meal together. The structure of the community meeting should be quite flexible in order to meet new needs.

The initial purpose of starting a second weekly meeting for the Grand Haven prayer group was to give members instruction in basic Christian living. Once the course was completed, the leaders team decided to encourage the members to continue meeting a second time each week in order to support each other in Christian growth and to deepen our love for one another. We changed the structure of the meeting after a year. To help people who lived near each other develop closer relationships, we established three large sharing groups of about twenty people each from distinct geographical areas. At each community meeting for the next year, the first hour was spent in a prayer meeting and the second hour was devoted to the sharing groups. This change allowed many people in the group to open their lives to others and to form new friendships.

At the end of the second year of community meetings, the leaders team decided that the purpose of the gathering was threefold: to create unity, to advance members to Christian maturity, and to develop commitment and personal relationships. Accordingly we structured the two-hour meeting so that each week there was a sharing in small groups (45 minutes), a prayer meeting (45 minutes), and a teaching (30 minutes). Each week, the leaders team planned the community gathering; sometimes elements were rearranged or dropped in order to accomplish what seemed to be the appropriate goal for specific meetings. Over the three-year period, various kinds of service meetings were scheduled before or after the community meetings. In its first year, for example, Life in the Spirit Seminar team meetings were held after the community meeting. The leaders team held a meeting for one hour before the gathering during the third year. The experience of the Grand Haven prayer group and of many others is that the most effective community meetings are those which are carefully tailored to the needs of the prayer group.

Sharing in Small Groups

Small group sharing is another important way to develop personal relationships among prayer group members. Many prayer groups provide opportunities for members to meet regularly with a few other people to share personally about their Christian lives. When all members are participating in such small groups, the prayer group becomes a stronger Christian environment in which members are building close friendships with one another.

Small group sharing is an essential source of growth for all Christians. Christians do not advance to maturity very well if they remain in isolation. Sharing with brothers and sisters encourages and hastens growth and is therefore one of our greatest resources in the Christian life. Personal sharing builds faith in all participants, provides opportunities for encouragement, creates an environment of trust, and helps people overcome obstacles they encounter.

Personal sharing builds faith in all participants. When I hear others share how God is working in their daily lives, I am reminded of his love for me and his invitation to put more faith in him. Over the past 10 years, I have participated in many small groups and found my faith increasing in response to someone else's experience. Regularly participating in a sharing group also builds faith by helping us maintain a sense of God's action in our daily lives. When I have not been part of a sharing group, I have not been very much aware of the Lord's presence and activity in my life. However, when I am sharing with others on a regular basis, I look at my life differently, seeking to see God working so that I might be able to share his work and his love with others. Participating in a small group calls forth a deeper faith in the Lord because it makes him more present to us.

Personal sharing provides us opportunities to receive and to give encouragement. In order to grow in holiness, individual Christians require the active support of brothers and sisters.

Many Christians are paralyzed by a poor self-image; for much of their lives they have heard from others that they are no good. A regular sharing group can be an effective antidote for the poisons of self-hatred which are frequently inflicted on us by our home, work, and school environments. Affection and encouragement from others sets us free from self-hate and allows us to center more clearly on serving the Lord. At the same time, participating in a sharing group can teach us how to express affection and give encouragement, something which few of us learn while growing up in our social environments. The more we learn to support one another, the more we will replace our ingrained sense of independence with a wholesome Christian interdependence.

Personal sharing creates an environment of trust among participants in a sharing group. Hearing others speak of their love for the Lord and of their personal strengths and weaknesses as Christians enables us to entrust our personal lives to them. When we know that a person has his heart set on loving God, we have a oneness of heart with him and a desire to develop a deeper bond with him. We become confident that we can speak intimately about how the Lord is working in us because we know the other person will respond with respect, interest, and understanding. In prayer groups where members are in regular sharing groups, the high level of mutual trust allows strong bonds of friendship and a system of healthy relationships to form and grow.

Personal sharing helps us overcome obstacles to growth in the Christian life. As people in sharing groups develop trust, they become more willing to discuss every area of their lives—including their failures and weaknesses. Openly admitting some wrongdoing or some weakness is often the first step to overcoming it. This has happened to me dramatically. Once I shared with a small group how I had become depressed because I had become angry over a minor incident. My openness—and their understanding and encouragement—allowed me to begin to overcome the problem. As long as I failed to admit my wrongdoing and weakness, the Spirit had a difficult time getting through to me, and I could not respond to his grace. Sharing about difficulties often invites others to speak about what they have learned in dealing with a similar problem. The experience of others in dealing with anger and depression has been a source of very practical instruction for me.

Accountability is another way in which sharing groups can help us deal with obstacles. For example, I have been able to master several personal problems by sharing them with others, telling them what I am doing to overcome them, and asking the group to hold me accountable by asking me about the problems regularly. If I am unusually silent about the problems in future meetings, they feel free to ask me how I am doing. By the grace of God, we can make each other stronger through regular personal sharing.

In summary, regular participation in sharing groups can be one of the most effective ways prayer groups have to build brotherhood among their members.

How to Develop Sharing Groups

Leaders teams should take a concern to help members form effective small groups for personal sharing. Some prayer groups simply provide a time before or after a regular gathering when sharing groups can meet. Some larger prayer groups with more organizational structure are forming "non-residential households." A non-residential household is a grouping of people, usually living near each other, who meet regularly during the week for personal sharing and some informal contact. Typically, these households meet for supper and have sharing afterwards. Other prayer groups have formed small sharing groups which meet as a regular part of their community meetings. No matter how small or new a prayer group, some kind of small group sharing is possible and ought to be attempted.

Usually, the leaders team should form the sharing groups by selecting members and designating an individual to lead the group. The criteria for forming groups varies according to the prayer group's needs. Some prayer groups develop random sharing groups, bringing together men and women of all ages. In particular, non-residential households are often composed of such mixed groups. On the other hand, some sharing groups have been formed with one type of person, usually to meet a particular need. These may include sharing groups for teen-agers, mothers, parents, and single parents. In one group, all the members who work in the medical professions meet together to share about their work. Prayer groups can set up both mixed and homogeneous sharing groups. Sharing groups can meet many needs, and leaders teams should approach them flexibly.

Leaders who form non-residential households should try not to isolate anyone. For example, the leaders team would usually relate a young man to a group that already has another young man, and so on. Some larger sharing groups, occasionally break down to allow the men and women to meet separately. The leaders team should work out a clear approach to forming groups before they start to do it. However, the leaders should also be flexible about their approach and imaginative about ideas for new groups.

The leaders of the sharing groups play a significant role; thus the leaders team should choose these people with care. The head of the sharing group should be able to take a responsibility for all of its activities. He or she leads the actual sharing, keeps the conversation moving, asks questions now and then, draws people out, and refocuses the sharing when it becomes sidetracked. The leader helps the group make plans, decide on activities, and takes a lead during informal events. In some very mature prayer goups, the head of a non-residential household may be asked to exercise some pastoral care for the people in his group. However, in most prayer groups, the head has concern only for the activities which the sharing group undertakes together.

Sharing groups should have a simple, definite pattern. All sharing groups should meet regularly. Gathering once a week is probably a minimum because less frequent meetings do not seem to give people enough contact with each other. Membership in sharing groups should be permanent enough to allow significant relationships to grow among participants and yet flexible enough to allow for changes when necessary. The pattern for an effective sharing group also includes having a designated leader, which was discussed above.

Building relationships requires that we share our lives with each other. Therefore, participants in small groups should share concretely about their own personal lives. Thus we should refrain from speaking about what is happening in the lives of others, unless there is some significant reason to. Discussing topics or Scripture may be very worthwhile activities for the sharing group, but they should not replace concrete personal sharing.

Sharing is concrete when the person provides sufficient detail so that the others are able to understand the significance of what he is saying. If a person simply shares that "I have been set free," the others are not able to benefit much from his experience. However, if he were to share how he overcame a serious problem with anger which had controlled him for the past year, the others would grow in faith and learn something about handling their own emotional weaknesses and problems. Members of the sharing group should help each other give concrete sharings by asking for specific details.

Some groups maintain the personal and concrete character of their sharing by following a set of questions. For example, the Grand Haven prayer group used the following questions in its sharing groups during community meetings: 1) In what ways were you aware of the Lord's presence or action in your life during the past week? 2) What has the Lord been teaching you in your prayer time or Scripture study this week? 3) In what ways has the Lord used you to serve others this past week? 4) What changes has the Lord been asking of you in order that you might grow in loving your brothers and sisters? Leaders teams can develop other questions which suit the needs of the members and which pinpoint the Lord's concerns for the prayer group. Responding to questions need not produce an artificial situation. As a framework to provide shape and direction, questions can be an effective means to lively personal interaction.

As in every other area, the more responsibly prayer groups approach forming sharing groups, the more effectively will they build with the Lord.

Commitment and Relationships

Calling forth a personal commitment to the prayer group has been another important element in developing Christian personal relationships in the charismatic renewal. As prayer groups continue to meet, the Lord seems to invite members to make some kind of commitment to each other. Members already share their fundamental commitment to Jesus and to each other as Christians, but they frequently discover the value of an additional commitment to come before the Lord as part of a specific local grouping. Such commitments, wherever they are made, strengthen the foundations for the renewal of Christian brotherhood.

One of the most significant steps in the growth of the Grand Haven prayer group came when the Holy Spirit led the members to freely announce that they loved each other and wanted to be together before the Lord. These professions of mutual love and commitment occurred spontaneously several times at community meetings of the Grand Haven group when no newcomers were present. After this happened several times, the leaders invited all members of the prayer group to affirm publicly, in their own words, their decision to be together as brothers and sisters. The statements which people made did not create commitment, but rather expressed the commitment we were already living. People in the Grand Haven group had drawn close together and had begun to support each other spiritually and materially long before they expressed this commitment to each other at prayer meetings.

The degree of commitment among prayer group members varies widely. Prayer groups should begin with a limited commitment, while remaining open to a deeper commitment if the Lord wills. Prayer groups normally should not call members to a degree of commitment which involves taking on a deep responsibility for each other's whole lives—including their spiritual, material, and psychological needs—as a close and loving family does for every member. The limited commitment which most prayer groups may undertake specifies only those things which all agree to have or do together. For example, the commitment to the Grand Haven prayer group at one point involved a simple affirmation of our fundamental commitment to the Lord and to each other, along with an agreement to attend meetings, to accept the leaders' authority over the group's functions, and to support the prayer group financially.

Leaders of prayer groups which begin to express commitments should continually remind the group that their commitments are not limited to an exclusive few but instead extend to all. Some people think, quite mistakenly, that personal commitment can extend to only a very few with whom we become intimately related. Indeed, intimacy is truly possible only with a few other people, but intimacy and commitment are not the same. Experience in prayer groups has shown that the same personal commitment can extend to twenty, fifty, a hundred, several hundred, a thousand, or even several thousand members. Intimacy involves deep personal sharing and is essential for our lives. Commitment involves a decision to be together with and support a body of people, some of whom we know intimately, many of whom we know only a little, but all of whom we love. Thus, prayer groups should remain open to including as many people as possible in their commitments.

The Holy Spirit will lead some, not all, prayer groups to publicly affirm their commitment to one another. Nevertheless, all prayer groups should focus on developing Christian personal relationships—on loving one another—rather than on meetings, on activities, or on being a prayer group. Members should see themselves first as brothers and sisters in the Lord and only secondarily as participants in a prayer group.

Prayer groups are investing a significant amount of energy in building effective structures—a trend this book encourages. But prayer groups should vigilantly resist the subtle tendency to make an idol of the prayer group's organization. Prayer meetings, informal contact, community meetings, sharing groups, and making commitments are of value only when they serve us in growing in love of God and each other.

7

Building Prayer Groups for Church Renewal

In winter, 1974, the planet Venus was visible in the morning sky. The star was the vanguard of the sun, announcing dawn's victory over night. I was fascinated by it, hardly able to keep my eyes on the road while driving to work.

What struck me most, however, was the impression this morning star made on my seven-year-old son, Paul. He discovered it one crisp morning when he poked his head out the front door to check on the weather. "Dad! Dad!" he exclaimed, "there's a big star out there! You should see it!" If I had not restrained him, Paul would have awakened the entire household to share the good news. Enchanted, he went back to the door to gaze at the star. Paul thought he had set his eyes on something no one had ever seen before and he wanted everyone to share his excitement.

As I reflected on Paul's behavior, it occurred to me that many of us in the charismatic renewal act the same way after being baptized in the Holy Spirit. We discover the Morning Star and we become enchanted with him. Our excitement grows as we come to know Jesus more. We act as though we were the first to have had any spiritual experience. To our new eyes, the church appears somewhat shabby and in need of repair. We want to jump in and renew it.

It was natural for my son to want everyone in the house to see the brilliant planet. But Paul was not the first to see the morning star. Millions of men had discovered it before him and were in their own way enchanted by it. Someday I know my son will realize this and will appreciate his experience all the more. In the same way, it is natural for us to want everyone, especially people in the church, to see Jesus as we have. Yet with all the newness of life we are undeniably experiencing, we are not the first to experience it. The life of the Spirit is the life of the church. Millions have lived it before us.

The Lord seems to intend to use charismatic prayer groups to make some contribution to the life of his church, but this contribution will not come automatically. To build with the Lord we must go with the Lord. To go with him, we must grasp his vision as clearly as we can. The first step toward sharing the Lord's vision is to grow in our understanding of the church and renewal. The more we see how the Lord has been working to build his church and give it new life, the more we will gaze at his work in awe. The more we appreciate the fullness of the church, the better will we be able to guide the charismatic renewal in accordance with the Lord's plans.

Grasping the Lord's Vision of the Church and Renewal

We sometimes have difficulty getting the church in proper focus because we have too narrow a view of it. The church is a many-faceted reality. We may see a part of it, and mistakenly think we see the whole. The first idea that comes to mind when we think of "church" is the local parish congregation and its buildings. The church must have a local expression, but to restrict our view of the church to the local assembly would be incomplete. Another common notion is to regard the church as a social and bureaucratic institution. Indeed, the church is a complex organization with officials, employees, and sets of rules to guide its members. The Lord gives his church leaders and laws so that we might grow to maturity as Christians in peace and order. But seeing the church as nothing more than an institution is to embrace a misleadingly restrictive view.

God has been working a long time to build his church. Even before he created us, it was the Father's plan to include man in the life of the Trinity. God is a community of persons—Father, Son and Holy Spirit—who share an intimate life of mutual love; the Father wanted man to share in this union. Adam's turning away from him did not divert the Father from this purpose. He was determined to have all mankind joined to him. The Lord chose to establish the church as a visible means of reuniting man with himself. He began to prepare the way by joining himself with Israel under the Old Covenant. The road was long and tortuous, for the Hebrew people proved fickle. A list of Israel's great men with approximate dates of when they lived gives some suggestion of the Lord's patient work:

1850 BC	Abraham
1250	Moses
1010	David
870	Elijah
740	Isaiah
27 AD	John the Baptist

After centuries of loving toil, the Father sent his Son Jesus with the mission of establishing the church. Jesus, the God-man, revealed in his person the wonderful design of God. By his death and resurrection, the Lord Jesus overwhelmed sin and death, our ancient enemies, and brought us into the divine community. The church was thus born on the cross and in the empty tomb. On the day of Pentecost the Lord took possession of the huddled band of disciples by filling them with the

Holy Spirit. From that time on, the Spirit has sanctified the church and strengthened it for the work of joining men to God.

How does God see the church? The New Testament presents a number of analogies which help us appreciate the mystery of the church more deeply. The church is the field of God, a choice vineyard which the Father himself cultivates (1 Cor. 3:9; John 15). In this field grows Christ Jesus, the True Vine, from whom we the branches are nourished with divine life. The church is God's building, his own dwelling place, built upon Jesus as the cornerstone and upon the foundation of the apostles and prophets (1 Cor. 3:9; Eph. 2:20-22). We are living stones fitted together in the new Temple of the Holy Spirit (1 Pet 2:5). The church is the Bride, the spouse of Christ, purified by his blood, nourished, sanctified, and protected by him in selfless love. In Christ's church we are married to the Lord himself (Eph. 5:22-33).

The church is the Body of Christ (Eph. 4:11-16); 1 Cor. 12:12-31). He is the head and we are the members, joined and fitted together so that at the Lord's direction every part might work toward building up the whole body to maturity. By the power of the Holy Spirit, who animates the body, every member exercises his diverse gifts to accomplish the purpose of extending the Lord's salvation to men. When Jesus walked the earth, men came to know the Father through his human presence. Now the church is equipped to do even more than Jesus did, for the man Jesus has become a corporate person extending his love and mercy through us, his members. The Lord desires to reach out through the Body of Christ to draw all mankind to himself. The scope of his design is cosmic and universal: he charges his church with nothing less than the restoration of all things in heaven and on earth in Christ Jesus (Eph. 1:10; 22-23).

When we focus on its divine constitution, it is not difficult to attribute to the church a false kind of completeness. We may readily conclude that the Founder established it in final form. However, history shows that from its beginning the church has had to cope with change, mistakes, and disaster. The New Testament church was a struggling assembly which could not have survived had it not made changes and reformed its life. Consider Paul's loving reprimand of the church at Corinth. He expected the whole community to address its problems, making appropriate changes in certain practices and to repent corporately by repairing their divisions and correcting abuses.

The church is a great ship offering rescue to men. Yet, like many less distinguished vessels, it has had to repair broken masts, replace rotting timbers, discipline rebellious crew members, retrieve those who fall overboard, weather storms, avoid near shipwreck, and alter course to avert new dangers. The church founded by Jesus according to his Father's plan and enlivened by his Holy Spirit has never been without a need for renewal.

To recognize the necessity for renewal is to recognize the humanity of the church. The church is a society of people who share in God's divinity, but it is a society of people all the same. Individual Christians are encased in time and space and are subject to improvement and deterioration. The church which Christians constitute shares their human condition. Our oneness with God does not erase our weakness, but gives us the power to cope with it. Similarly, the divine elements in the church do not destroy its human characteristics. The Lord enhances the natural qualities of his Bride; he does not obliterate them. Individual Christians, lured by evil tendencies within and temptations from without, sometimes turn from the Lord and must take steps to repair their wrongdoing. Daily we must present our humanity to the Lord for transformation. The whole church is in this situation too. Thus, church renewal is the process of the human church responding to the invitation of the Lord to make changes, to repair wrongdoing, and to present itself to him for transformation.

Bringing new life to the church is the Lord's work, but he invites us to share in it. We can be sidetracked from cooperating with him if we plunge in and try to reshape the church according to our own whims. We need to submit ourselves to the Lord so that he can shape our efforts.

The Charismatic Renewal and Church Renewal

Over the centuries the Lord has chosen to use movements in the church to generate renewal. Movements have helped rally the church in the face of new challenges, bringing new life and new hope. They have succored the church when it was beleaguered by political enemies. They have been a source of spiritual vitality when hope was wearing thin. The reform movements of the eleventh century fostered by centers such as Cluny provided the initial impetus behind papal efforts to rescue the church from the grasp of feudal overlords. The movements came none too soon, for the church was suffocating. The Dominican and Franciscan movements refreshed the thirteenth century church by calling townspeople to live the gospel life simply and in deep personal union with God.

The history of earlier movements can help us understand the place of the charismatic renewal in the renewal of the church. The experience of the early monastic movement is particularly instructive. In the fourth century, thousands of Christians in the eastern Roman Empire began to respond to God's call to give up their lives in order to find him. Men and women abandoned their homes and jobs to dwell in the solitude of the desert, sometimes as hermits and sometimes in informal or formal communities. The movement was characterized by the encounter with God in perpetual quiet prayer, poverty, chastity, submission to elders, love of the brothers, and hospitality.

While they conducted no programs of evangelization, the monks were nonetheless superb evangelists. By the witness of their lives, they proclaimed the gospel in a way that brought refreshment to the church. The monks did not need to say a word. Their lives—given to God and to each other—persuaded thousands of Christians in the church that the Kingdom of God was within. This was a timely lesson, for Christians in the post-Constantinian era needed to rediscover the inner depths of their oneness with the Lord. Through the example of the brothers in the desert, many Christians learned how to pray. The monastic movement was not a new church. It was a renewal movement that subordinated itself to the church. Ultimately the monastic movement ceased to be a movement and was incorporated into the church's life, providing leadership and spiritual education for thousands.

The experience of the recent liturgical movement in the twentieth century also helps to bring the charismatic renewal into focus. The goal of the liturgical movement was the restoration of worship in the Catholic Church. In particular, it sought to bring the mass to the people. Beginning several decades ago among a handful of scholars and pastors, the movement gradually involved thousands of priests, religious, and laymen. Through books, journals, talks, conferences, and remodeled worship services, the participants developed widespread concern among Catholics for the restoration of the liturgy. The movement accumulated vast wisdom about the history and nature of Christian worship, and gained a great deal of pastoral sense about helping groups of all kinds give corporate praise to the Lord. The liturgical movement peaked in the early 1960s. Vatican Council II integrated the liturgical movement's wisdom and objectives into the entire church by laying the foundations for a thorough reformation of the liturgy. Since the church itself assumed the initiative, a movement with a separate identity was no longer needed. The liturgical movement had reached its goal—starting the liturgical renewal of the Catholic Church. This does not mean that all the work has been done. To the contrary, the work of liturgical renewal has just begun. However, the need for a separate movement to generate interest in the renewal of worship has passed.

Three lessons drawn from the examples of early monasticism and the liturgical movement are useful in understanding the role of the charismatic renewal in the renewal of the church.

1) *Movements for church renewal are not ends in themselves.* Movements exist to contribute to the life of the church and come to an end where the church accepts these contributions. Realizing this should help us shed a false sense of importance we sometimes place on the charismatic renewal and help us understand its real importance. The goal of the charismatic renewal is to bring a charismatic renewal to the entire church. The Lord intends all the valuable gifts he has given the charismatic renewal—personal renewal through being baptized in the Spirit; the renewal of charisms such as prophecy; the prayer meeting; the prayer group; and other new forms such as households and communities—to nourish the life of his entire church. The church is already incorporating the elements of the renewal into its general life. The more this happens, the sooner the charismatic renewal can cease to exist as a movement.

2) *For a time, a movement needs to maintain its separate identity within the church.* The monks were able to call other Christians to personal renewal by separating themselves from the ordinary environment and building new forms of Christian living in the North African desert. The liturgical movement needed its separate identity to create a situation which prepared the church for a full-scale reform of worship. Had there been no liturgical movement, Vatican Council II would not have been able to take up the question of renewing the liturgy in the way it did.

For the present, the charismatic renewal must continue to develop as a movement in the church. There is a great deal of work to be done to develop prayer groups, to help others who want to be baptized in the Holy Spirit, to help each other become mature Christians. Since the renewal is for the church, we should remain actively subordinate to the church. But we should not be too quick to de-emphasize important characteristic elements of the movement in the interest of relating the charismatic renewal to the church. For example, in my judgment, we would be mistaken to stop speaking about "being baptized in the Spirit" and "speaking in tongues" for the purpose of making the charismatic renewal more acceptable to certain elements in the church. To do this may even make the charismatic renewal completely inaccessible to people because it would seem like a movement with no distinctive characteristics. Like early monasticism and the liturgical movement, the charismatic renewal should relate respectfully to the church while at the same time developing the special features of renewal which the Lord has given it. To do this, is to build with the Lord to renew his church.

3) Movements successfully foster church renewal when they maintain their concern for personal spiritual renewal. The early monks dedicated themselves to living for God daily, and to helping one another learn to pray, to cope with problems, and to mature as Christians. Anthony, one of the founders of the movement, had no idea that he was starting something; he simply wanted to respond to the Lord in the quiet places. Even when the monastic movement acquired some organization, it never strayed from its foundational concern to bring men to dwell in prayerful harmony with God.

Participants in the charismatic renewal should understand that authentic church renewal is rooted in personal spiritual renewal. The church lives in its individual members. Its holiness grows as the individual members grow in holiness. If prayer group members want to renew the church, the place to begin is in our own hearts. If prayer groups want to renew the church, they ought to become better prayer groups. By their presence in the church, prayer groups which help us turn to the Lord and live for him already constitute a vital renewal. This does not mean that prayer groups should turn in on themselves. Prayer groups are training us in brotherhood and service that spill over into our normal relationships with the church. Church renewal is new life. It is new life which charismatic prayer groups have discovered and continue to foster. Building prayer groups with the Lord, then, is building church renewal.

Relating Prayer Groups to the Church

Prayer groups hold a key position in feeding the experience of the charismatic renewal into the mainstream of the church. They have made the renewal present everywhere; they will continue to be the main instruments for relating the charismatic movement to the church.

The prayer group is well suited to perform this service. It evokes enough commitment from participants to maintain some kind of Christian communitarian environment. Yet a prayer group does not have so much of a common life that members must pull back from everything else. People can count on the prayer group's gathering regularly for praise, sharing, and mutual encouragement. However, the commitment of members need not be structured in a way which dramatically reduces the participation of laymen in their parishes, or of religious in their communities. In a well-organized prayer group, a handful of leaders will find it necessary to devote the major part of their time and energy—beyond their commitments to family, job, and personal needs—to building the group. For them, the involvement in the local parish will be minimal, consisting of church attendance, tithing, occasional religious education meetings, social events, and the like. However, most participants in the prayer group should be able to define their priorities so that they can give themselves to the Lord's work in both parish and prayer group. Prayer group members should help each other sort out personal priorities, seeing to it that they are maintaining a concern for the church.

Whether prayer groups fulfill their role of bringing the whole church into a charismatic renewal will depend upon how wisely we build the groups in relationship to the church and how well we form the attitudes of the participants toward the church.

Prayer groups must carefully consider their manner of relating to local parishes and congregations. Groups should maintain good communications with local church leaders by sharing what the Lord is doing and keeping them informed about activities. Many bishops have appointed official liaison persons with whom leaders should be in frequent contact. Prayer groups that are a part of the charismatic renewal should encourage participants to be faithful to their church. Catholics should be unashamedly loyal to their bishops, actively subordinating themselves to their authority. Other Christians need to maintain the same loyalty and submission to the governing bodies of their churches.

Prayer groups should encourage participants to become active members of their churches. This means doing something more than the minimum expected of any church member. Service is a way of expressing brotherly love. Many parishes sponsor worthwhile activities like hospital visitation programs, clothing centers for the poor, or basic adult education for the underpriviliged. The Lord wants some members to spend themselves in this kind of service. Prayer group members may assume leadership positions on parish councils or school boards. If we do, we must conduct ourselves as servants, showing respect to church members who may not be involved in the prayer group and not attempting to force our own way. If we have a choice between something which will happen without us (being a reader at worship) and some unsung menial task which nobody likes (cleaning the church regularly) choosing the menial task is the loving thing to do.

In general, we should serve in our parishes without becoming overextended. We should pass over those parish activities that seem less important in favor of those where we sense the Lord would have us work. While the Lord does not want us to serve in every parish activity, neither does he want us to condemn or criticize parish activities that we do not actively support. Our service in our parishes should be discerning, and also governed by love.

Leaders teams should take a responsibility for forming the attitudes of participants toward the church. There should be frequent teaching in the prayer group on the nature of the church and the correct relationship between the charismatic renewal and the church. This teaching can be extremely effective. Once an elder from a local Protestant church who also belonged to the Grand Haven group told me that many local Protestant leaders respected the prayer group's stance regarding the church. They appreciated our persistent opposition to the false notion that the prayer group is the "true church." They also liked our oft-repeated reminders that there are no class distinctions among Christians—the first-class Christians who speak in tongues and the lower-class groups who do not. Many people easily pick up such false and divisive attitudes. Through sound teaching and personal correction when necessary, we need to call each other to renounce these views.

Leaders teams should discourage participants from regarding the church simply as a target for evangelism and renewal. Keeping the true nature of the church in view ought to foster respect for God's plan. One particular weakness that should be corrected in prayer group members is a tendency to criticize elements of their church's life that do not seem to have an explicit basis in the New Testament. Some people have no trouble seeing how the Holy Spirit has changed their prayer group, and yet cannot see that the same Spirit has guided the church to change in response to circumstances unknown in the apostolic age. Some aspects of the church that seem to depart from New Testament practices may be signs of life rather than death.

Prayer groups should encourage their members to refrain from using special in-group jargon which is a frequent cause of misunderstanding in local churches. "The Lord laid it on my heart;" "Is Father X in the Spirit?"; "Have you got the 'baptism?' " are examples of expressions that are offensive or confusing. Statements such as these do not accurately describe our experience, and they cannot help others desire to share the same experience themselves. A person who hears a friend say that "the Lord laid it on my heart to speak to you," is very likely to be confused. He probably thinks that the Lord has never laid anything on his heart, and hopes that he never does. We should encourage each other to speak plainly, avoiding problematic expressions. Eliminating jargon protects us from appearing to be an in-group and helps us relate properly to the church.

Ecumenism

For centuries, Christianity has been scandalously divided into many churches. However, the Lord, especially in the twentieth century, has been working faithfully to re-establish the church's original unity. The charismatic renewal is making a substantial contribution to the progress of Christian unity. Official church bodies have made significant steps toward reunion through theological dialogue, but little progress has been made at the grass roots in parishes and congregations where vital work of restoring unity must happen. Here is where the charismatic renewal offers new hope. In the prayer groups of the charismatic renewal, Christians from many different denominations are finding a new relationship with the

Lord and entering into solid brotherly relationships with each other. As they submit anew to the Lordship of Jesus and are empowered afresh by the Holy Spirit, Protestants, Catholics, Evangelicals, Orthodox, and Pentecostals are discovering that they can love one another in spite of the differences among them. Along with this great promise for ecumenism, there are also dangers. Thus, prayer groups must exercise great care to conduct ecumenical relationships properly.

Authentic ecumenism demands that members of ecumenical prayer groups be openly committed to their churches. Loving one another does not require that we blur our denominational differences. Leaders teams should encourage participants to center on our common love for Jesus and on the power of the Holy Spirit who makes us one. But at the same time, leaders should carefully instruct members about the importance of remaining faithful to the authority of their churches and to their churches' teaching. Frequent teaching on having a right relationship with our church will help prayer groups maintain a proper ecumenical stance which will not slide into religious indifferentism. Prayer group leaders should also teach against false ecumenical notions such as come-outism, which calls people out of their churches into a false, invisible communion with others who have abandoned their churches.

Prayer group members should be sensitive and patient in their ecumenism. Sensitivity requires that teaching and sharing never be so biased as to be offensive to Christians from different traditions. Also, peripheral pious practices and doctrines from any denomination should not be emphasized in our prayer meetings.

Patience demands that ecumenical prayer groups accept the present state of division among Christian churches as a fact, while praying and hoping for reunion. Members should never try to force a greater unity among each other than the Lord has created. For example, the discipline of many churches prohibits intercommunion. Our hearts may yearn to declare our oneness by taking communion together, but the fact of division in many cases still prevents it. The right behavior for the prayer group participant is to accept the degree of unity the Lord has given us now, obey the discipline of his church, and pray earnestly for the day when we can all partake of the one bread and the one cup.

All prayer groups, even those which are exclusively Catholic, Protestant, or Orthodox in membership, should become truly ecumenical at heart. We should all be open to praying with brothers and sisters from different Christian backgrounds. We should all undertake to pray and fast for the reunion of Christianity. Ecumenical prayer groups should take their role seriously and learn how to grow in loving other Christians while remaining faithful to their churches.

In short, prayer groups that desire to be in right relationship with the church and to bring it new life will teach members to rest their attitudes and behavior with the Lord's new command that we love one another in the same way that he loved us.

Conclusion

In the early days of the charismatic renewal, a survey was taken at a Michigan day of renewal. To the question "What has being baptized in the Holy Spirit meant in your life?," one of the leaders answered ironically, "a lot of work!" When the charismatic renewal broke out, many had expected the Holy Spirit to do all the work. Only a short time elapsed before we discovered that while the Spirit was very active, we had to work with him.

Much work remains to be done in building the charismatic renewal and the church. Our energy will not be wasted, for the dwelling place we are constructing is the Lord's own house and the Lord himself is the master builder. Our task is to spend ourselves joyfully, building with him.

For Further Study

Prayer groups and leaders teams who wish to explore topics more deeply should consult the following list of selected books and cassettes.

CHAPTER ONE: BUILDING WITH THE LORD

Basic Christian Maturity. Word of Life, 1975. W-6002: Cassette album with leaders guide, $22.50; leaders guide only, $1.95.

A series of eight talks that present a vision for living as mature Christians. Talks 2, 3, and 4 on Christian love, faith and guidance, respectively, develop principles presented in this chapter.

Clark, Steve. *Growing in Faith*. Word of Life, 1972. 61 pp. $.95

A helpful, short essay on how to trust God to act.

Clark, Steve. *Knowing God's Will*. Word of Life, 1974. 66 pp. $.95.

Advice on how to obtain God's guidance for your life and for your prayer group.

Martin, Ralph. *Unless the Lord Build the House . . .* Ave Maria Press, 1971. 63 pp. $.75.

A moving presentation of the Christian ideal in building the church and Christian groups.

CHAPTER TWO: DEVELOPING LEADERS TEAMS

Clark, Steve. *Building Christian Communities: Strategy for Renewing the Church.* Ave Maria Press, 1972. 189 pp. $1.50.

A significant description of the kind of leadership necessary for bringing renewal to the church. Prayer group leaders will especially benefit from the sections on the environmental approach to building groups, on keeping the whole view, and on pastoral leadership.

Coleman, Robert E. *The Master Plan of Evangelism.* Fleming H. Revell Company, 1963. 126 pp. $1.50.

A study of the principles the Lord used to develop the New Testament leadership for the church.

Nee, Watchman. *The Normal Christian Worker.* Church Book Room, 1965. 133 pp. $1.75.

A convincing and convicting description of the character traits necessary for effective Christian leaders.

Synan, Vinson, *The Holiness Pentecostal Movement in the United States.* W. Eerdmans, 1971. 248 pp. $5.95 (hardbound only).

Prayer group leaders can profit from reflecting on this objective historical study of the merits and mistakes of leaders of the classical Pentecostal movement.

Cassettes:

Harvey, Jerry and Claire. *Help for New Prayer Group Leaders.* Charismatic Renewal Cassettes, A-1120. $4.95.

Offers basic advice on common problems of prayer group development: spiritual gifts, teaching, leadership, services, youth.

Martin, George. *The Gift of Administration.* Charismatic Renewal Cassettes, A-1128. $4.95.

Administration of practical needs is a vital support to the pastoral leadership of growing prayer groups. Martin defines the gift of administration and presents many helpful principles for exercising it.

Spiritual Leadership. Cassette album and study guide. Word of Life, W-5001. $19.95.

A basic vision of service that has been developed in the charismatic renewal. The four talks are: "Essential Elements for Building Prayer Groups"; "The Goal: Building Christian Brotherhood"; "What is Spiritual Leadership?"; and "Spiritual Growth for Leaders".

CHAPTER THREE: BRINGING PRAYER MEETINGS TO LIFE

Cavnar, Jim. *Prayer Meetings.* Dove Publications, 1969. 36 pp. $.50.

A basic explanation of the nature and purposes of prayer meetings.

Cavnar, Jim. *Participating in Prayer Meetings*. Word of Life, 1974. 61 pp. $.95.

A manual for prayer group members.

Clark, Steve. *Spiritual Gifts*. Dove Publications, 1969. 35 pp. $.50.

A brief definition and description of the spiritual gifts and their operation in the Christian life.

Songs of Praise. Word of Life, 1975. 96 pp. $2.00.

Seventy-nine songs for use in charismatic prayer meetings. Songbook includes lyrics, melody and guitar chords.

Cassettes:

Cavnar, Jim. *How to Form a Music Group*. Word of Life, W-1016. $4.95.

Explains the role of a music ministry in leading songs at prayer meetings.

Cavnar, Jim. *Sing to the Lord a New Song*. Word of Life, W-1009. $4.95.

Principles for a wise use of music to enhance worship in prayer meetings.

CHAPTER FOUR: HELPING OTHERS RECEIVE NEW LIFE

Clark, Steve. *Baptized in the Spirit.* Dove Publications, 1970. 76 pp. $.60.

A background essay on the experience of being baptized in the Holy Spirit. Life in the Spirit Seminar teams will find it helpful for understanding the pastoral approach recommended in the "Team Manual".

Finding New Life in the Spirit. Word of Life, 1973 46 pp. $.50.

A guidebook for participants in Life in the Spirit Seminars. The booklet includes daily Scripture meditations for the seven weeks of the seminar.

The Life in the Spirit Seminars Team Manual. Word of Life, 1973. 183 pp. $1.95.

A prayer group's handbook for helping people receive a release of the Holy Spirit. The manual is a complete guide for presenting the seminars.

Cassettes:

Clark, Steve. *What is the Good News?* Word of Life, W-1011. $4.95.

This presentation of the core of the gospel proclamation will help Life in the Spirit Seminar teams understand the evangelistic content of seminars.

Clark, Steve. *What Does it Mean to be Saved?, Key Pastoral Issues*. Word of Life, W-1012. $4.95.

An explanation of the scriptural way of salvation: repent, believe, and be baptized. The talk shows how individuals make or renew contact with God.

Gavriledes, Doug. *Yielding to the Gift of Tongues*. Charismatic Renewal Cassettes, C-136. $4.95.

The value of the gift of tongues and how to receive it.

Ghezzi, Bert. *Helping People Appropriate New Life*. Charismatic Renewal Cassettes, A-1084. $4.95.

Practical advice for discussion leaders in Life in the Spirit Seminars.

Ghezzi, Bert and Doug Gavrilides. *Life in the Spirit Seminars: Teaching and Dyanmics*. Charismatic Renewal Cassettes, A-1071. $4.95.

How to use the team manual for Life in the Spirit Seminars; the vision behind the seminars; adapting the seminars to the local situation; and how to pray for people to be baptized in the Holy Spirit.

Life in the Spirit Seminars. Charismatic Renewal Cassettes, LSB. $15.00.

The talks from the seminars as presented in The Word of God, an ecumenical Christian community in Ann Arbor, Michigan. This series provides teachers with model presentations.

CHAPTER FIVE: PROVIDING TEACHING

Basic Christian Maturity. Word of Life, W-6002. Cassette album with leaders guide, $22.50; leaders guide only, $1.95.

Eight talks from "The Foundations of Christian Living" series developed by The Word of God, an ecumenical Christian community, Ann Arbor, Michigan. The first four talks describe some of the essential characteristics of the mature Christian and the last four talks give instruction about dealing with the sources of the problems Christians face. Leaders teams may either use the album and guide to develop their own teaching, or play the cassettes for their prayer groups.

Cassettes:

Yocum, Bruce. *Developing Teaching*. Charismatic Renewal Cassettes, A-1118. Set, $8.95.

Understanding the role of teaching in prayer groups; how to develop basic instruction in the practicalities of the Christian life.

Yocum, Bruce. *Giving Teaching*. Charismatic Renewal Cassettes, A-1125. $4.95.

A discussion of the goal of Christian teaching; how to adapt teaching to the local situation; advice on the preparation and evaluation of teachings.

CHAPTER SIX: MAKING LOVE YOUR AIM

Lewis, C.S. *The Four Loves.* Harcourt, Brace, Jovanovich, Inc. 1960. 192 pp. $2.45.

A description of the four basic kinds of human love—affection, friendship, erotic love and the love of God.

Cassettes:

Clark, Steve. *Christian Personal Relationships.* Word of Life, W-3003. Set, $8.95.

Explains Chrisitan love as self-sacrificing commitment to others. Detailed advice on building committed personal relationships in prayer groups.

CHAPTER SEVEN: BUILDING PRAYER GROUPS FOR CHURCH RENEWAL

Clark, Steve. *Where Are We Headed?* Word of Life, 1973. 80 pp. $1.25.

Guidelines for developing prayer groups and establishing right relationships between the charismatic renewal and the church.

Martin, George, *An Introduction to the Catholic Charismatic Renewal.* Word of Life, 1975. 15 pp. $.15; $9.00/100 copies.

A pamphlet which defines the Catholic charismatic renewal and answers commonly asked questions. A helpful summary of what the Catholic hierarchy has said about the renewal.

New Covenant, February 1976. "How Can Prayer Groups Serve the Church?"

This issue presents a series of instructive articles about the role of the prayer group in bringing new life to the church.

Ranaghan, Kevin. *The Lord, the Spirit and the Church.* Word of Life, 1973. 63 pp. $.95.

A brief instruction on developing right relationships with the church.

Theological and Pastoral Orientations on the Catholic Charismatic Renewal. Word of Life, 1974. 71 pp. $2.00.

Prepared at Malines, Belgium, May 21-26, 1974 by theologians and pastoral leaders, this document examines the theological basis for the charismatic renewal and reviews pastoral practices in the movement.

Cassettes:

Clark, Steve. *Advice to Catholics on Ecumenism.* Charismatic Renewal Cassettes, A-1105. $4.95.

Advice on developing ecumenical prayer groups.

Martin, Ralph. *Rebuild My Church.* Charismatic Renewal Cassettes, A-1160. $4.95.

A prophetic report on the signs of renewal in the church and an exhortation to remain open to what the Lord is doing in the church.

Ranaghan, Kevin. *Attitudes Toward Ecumenism.* Charismatic Renewal Cassettes, A-1096. $4.95.

Advice on developing sound attitudes and approaches to ecumenism from a Catholic perspective.

McFadden, Jim. *Reordering Priorities*. Word of Life, W-1017. $4.95.

Guidelines for sorting out priorities in our lives such as family, work, church, prayer group. How to evaluate commitments and how to organize use of time effectively.

Note: All books and cassettes listed in this section can be purchased from:

Charismatic Renewal Services
Drawer A
Notre Dame, Indiana 46556

New Covenant subscriptions and back issues are available from:

New Covenant
Box 102
Ann Arbor, Michigan 48107